Little Tenement
on the Volga

Little Tenement
on the Volga

by C. S Walton

Garrett County Press
www.gcpress.com

non-fiction

For more information: Garrett County Press

828 Royal St. #248

New Orleans, LA 70116

www.gcpress.com

GCPress books are printed on acid free paper.
Text and cover designed by Gail Carter.

LIBRARY OF CONGRESS CATALOG CARD NUMBER: 00-133023

ISBN: 1-891053-78-7

First Edition   2001

CONTENTS

PREFACE

The Edge of Civilization

This book tells the stories of a handful of people who live in the Volga city of Samara. Their personal dramas are reflected countless times throughout Russia. For nearly half a century these people lived behind a double iron curtain, as their city was one of the many areas of the former Soviet Union closed to westerners.

Samara not only occupies the geographical margins of Europe; at times in history its inhabitants have been pushed over the limits of what we like to call civilization. The civil war of 1919-1920 created a famine that reduced people to cannibalism. Today cannibalism has returned in a metaphorical sense as former communists grow rich by dismantling and selling off the state's resources.

I landed in Samara through a chance meeting with a refugee in London. Valentina said she had grown tired of living on the edge of civilization. She gave me an invitation to the home town she had chosen to escape.

I am grateful to have had this rare opportunity—for a westerner—of experiencing Russian society in transition, and would like to thank all those who talked to me about their lives. I feel especially blessed by the friendship of Lina Ivanovna Shatalova.

Little Tenement
on the Volga

Number Four, Specialist Alley

A small boy pointed at the portrait of Lenin hanging on the waiting-room wall.

"Who's that, Granny?"

"That's Lenin, dear."

"Who's Lenin?"

After a moment's reflection the old lady replied:

"He was a president, son."

I was in the Department of Visas and Foreign Affairs to register my temporary domicile in Samara. The waiting-room gave me the impression of stepping back into the 19th century. It was almost dark, and quite silent except for the buzz of flies and the clack of a typewriter coming from an inner office. Wooden benches were crammed with peasant women in headscarves and shabby men in felt boots. I asked: "Who's last in the queue?"

Silence. I repeated the question in a stentorian voice. A few weather-beaten faces looked up, but no one answered. Each lumpy face radiated *priterpelost*—a characteristically Russian expression for patience and the capacity to endure.

In frustration I strode past the row of supplicants and barged through a forbidding door. It opened into a calm and sunny office. A pair of plump ladies in fluffy jumpers sat behind their desks stirring glasses of tea. They looked up in annoyance at having their peace disturbed. I announced that

I was a foreigner who wanted a *propiska*. As I had expected, they were pleased to have such an unprecedented distraction. I praised the beauties of the city while one of the ladies galvanised herself to pick up her pen.

A family group was gathered around a farther desk. The younger members were encouraging a man of about 60 to sign a paper. His face was twisted into a grimace as he drooled onto his shiny black suit. A girl directed his hand along the page. I was wondering what rights the poor fellow was signing away when one of the officials interrupted my thoughts.

"This document must be copied. Go to that side-office over there."

I obeyed, sticking my head through a hatch in a cubbyhole and addressing the clerk within. She snatched my papers and scanned through them. Seeing my nationality she barked: "This paper must be translated!"

"But it's already written in Russian—otherwise you wouldn't have been able to read it!"

She shoved the document back into my hands and slammed the shutter down. I knew I should open my purse and wave a couple of dollar bills through the glass, but I was suddenly overcome with bitter fatigue.

I seized my papers and stomped out through the waiting-room of dead souls. No one stirred in the gloom.

Back home in Specialist Alley I let off steam to my neighbours.

"You see, this is how we lived and how we still live," they replied. "The bureaucracy stamps on us at every turn. They have it all sewn up. We can do absolutely nothing for ourselves. Our only recourse is bribery. Bureaucrats increase the number of rules and regulations in order to get paid for breaking them.

"We know that place. It's always the same. Those peasants

in the waiting-room have probably been there so long they have forgotten why they came. They visit the city twice in their lives, for marriage certificates and death certificates. Now you see what the Soviet system has done to our people. The bureaucracy weighs down on us from cradle to grave. There is nothing we can do except wait and endure."

Samara, or Kuibyshev as it was known from the thirties until 1991, lies on the river Volga 600 miles east of Moscow. Locals call it the Russian Chicago, in honour of its industrial base and rampant gangsterism. From 1946 to 1991 Samara was designated so secret that Volga cruise-ships carrying foreigners could only pass its shores at night. Some districts are still off-limits to civilians.

In comparison to Moscow and St. Petersburg this region seems to be frozen in a time-warp. Its inhabitants may design space rockets, but their way of life is firmly rooted in the past. Kuibyshev was a self-contained provincial city; only those citizens with impeccable Party credentials travelled abroad. Most never ventured further than Moscow, and then only for shopping or school sight-seeing trips.

Founded in the 16th century as a fortified trading post on the Volga, Samara is now the country's sixth-largest city with a population of one and a half million. It occupies a spit of land at the confluence of the Volga and Samarka rivers. The town centre is a relic of pre-revolution Russia with ornate department stores of crumbling stucco and an art nouveau chocolate factory. The embankment is lined with fin-de-siècle merchants' mansions. Behind these lie streets of painted wooden houses, their eaves and window frames carved like starched lace. These houses are crammed with refugees, immigrants from other republics, the poor and the down-and-out.

Most of Samara's residents live in dreary suburbs—*micro-raioni*—of identical tower blocks. From the distance of the Volga's far shore greater Samara holds the promise of a Mediterranean coastal city, its blocks gleaming white against fresh blue skies. Up close, they dissolve into honeycombs of pale grey concrete, their balconies shielded by corrugated plastic: great cliffs of vertical shanty dwellings.

Interspersed among the *micro-raioni* are clusters of private sector housing, remnants of former villages engulfed by the spreading city. These areas are considered undesirable and dangerous; the ramshackle wooden buildings are overcrowded and lack sanitation. Roughest of all is an industrial suburb centred on a giant aluminium plant. This is the sinister *Bezimyanka*, literally "nameless place," built by German prisoner-of-war labour.

Samara's citizens claim they used to be third priority for a US nuclear strike. The city was primarily devoted to the manufacture of tanks, missiles and military aircraft. The most secret weapons were produced in a labyrinth of underground works.

The city is built on skeletons of the Soviet past. When workmen dug out two artificial lakes in Gagarin park they found thousands of bones of people shot by the NKVD in the thirties. There is a forlorn graveyard by the Samarka, a resting place for local boys killed in Afghanistan. Below Samara are the satellite towns of Novokuibyshevsk and Chapaevsk. Their cemeteries are filled with the corpses of workers killed in building accidents, chemical and gas explosions. Little attention was paid to safety measures in the course of post-war industrial expansion.

The grimmest period of Samara's history was in the early 1920s. The middle Volga region was hit by a famine caused by crop failure and the civil war. Lenin and the Bolshevik government were initially reluctant to accept foreign aid, but eventually relented. As correspondent for the *Manchester Guardian,* the writer Arthur Ransome sent back harrowing reports from the area. A relief fund was organised in Britain and elsewhere. While it is touching to read the list of donors, the contributions of "An old Jewish pauper", "Ian and Cherry of Manchester" and others failed to prevent up to five million deaths. Orphaned children roamed the countryside. French relief workers sent back photographs of Samaran cannibals flanked by human remains.

The drowned city of Stavropol lies a few miles up the Volga. Like General Franco, Stalin was keen on damming rivers to create vast reservoirs. As the waters swallowed the old city a new one, Toliatti, was raised beside the dam. Toliatti is admired by the region's inhabitants because unlike Samara, it is disconnected from the past. This city compares itself to Detroit as it exists to produce *Zhiguli* cars.

When I first arrived in Samara I rented a modern flat in a twelve-storey block indistinguishable from hundreds of others built since the 1970s. From this time onwards country folk poured into the city, attracted by urban amenities and jobs in the defence industry. After the break-up of the old Soviet Union the demand for housing intensified as Russians return from the former republics. An elderly teacher complained that she could only find room in a student hostel when she returned from Frunze. She was incensed by what she saw as Kirghiz ingratitude.

"The Soviet government encouraged us to move out there. I thought I was doing my duty. We even gave them an alphabet. Having been trained by us they now fill professional positions with their own people."

It seemed almost immoral to have my own two room flat, which would normally house a family of four or five. Residents of *kommunalnii* (communal) flats spend their lives scheming to acquire one of these shoe boxes. Some die still dreaming of a flat of their own.

Yet the remoteness and dreariness of the area in which I lived depressed me, so after a while I moved to a *kommunalnaya* in the city centre. Number Four, Specialist Alley had been built in the 1870s as a block of six apartments for merchants' families. After the revolution these had been partitioned into communal flats of ten or twelve rooms leading off a central corridor. Each room housed a couple or a family. Each flat contained one kitchen and one washroom. The kitchens were equipped with two sinks and three gas stoves. Clothes and sheets were washed here in metal tubs. Water had to be heated up on the stoves. The washrooms contained two lavatories and two cold water taps over a trough. Some residents kept their personal wooden toilet seats hanging from nails on the wall. There was always a queue for the washroom in the morning.

One unshaded bulb illuminated the entrance to my *kommunalnaya*. Inside, the corridor led off into gloom. Colours faded to the muted tones of an old sepia print. At the far end of the corridor flannelette drawers dangled from washing lines. Hulking chests piled with yellowing newspapers stood against the walls. Great doors padded with peeling brown vinyl opened into individual rooms. The air stank of rotting fish left out for the semi-feral cats that inhabited the stairwell.

It was hard to believe that 75 years had passed since the Party district housing committee had requisitioned the block, partitioned the flats, and allocated them to workers' families. This temporary arrangement had stuck, while time passed the inhabitants by. My neighbour in the next room had been born in the building 67 years ago, and expected to die there.

Every day at seven I was awakened by the sound of the neighbour's radio through the dividing wall. After a blast of mechanical bird-tweeting a hearty woman would urge the nation to rise to its feet and exercise. She sounded as though she was just bursting to call us "comrades"; she made me feel like Winston Smith.

Anyone who has ever shared a flat could imagine the tensions within a *kommunalnaya*, where residents do not even select their co-tenants. A tiny room is not conducive to happy family life; still less when the family knows that every fight will be overheard and subjected to minute discussion by neighbours glad of a distraction from their own problems.

Not wanting to be drawn into kitchen politics, I spent most of my time in my room. I did not join the other women when they gathered in front of the television in a neighbour's room for their daily escape into Mexican soap operas. The transmission of these wildly melodramatic soaps is probably the most popular feature of post-communist Russia. My neighbours said they wanted to see how people lived in Mexico. When I suggested that blonde ladies in palacios were not typical representatives of the Mexican population they looked at me sceptically, as though I was a purveyor of communist propaganda.

On Friday and Saturday nights my elderly male neighbours would drink heavily. If they met me on my way to the lavatory they were wont to put their hands on their hearts, bow, and mumble compliments in German. I circumvented their gallantry by buying a plastic bucket. I would creep out and empty it in the early hours of the morning while the *kommunalnaya* slept.

I loved my narrow room with its faded honeysuckle wallpaper marked around the skirting board with the brown splodges of squashed cockroaches. A man who had helped arrange my Russian visa found me the room. Boris was a small time black-marketeer and speculator. He said he lived as splendidly as Raskolnikov—Dostoevsky's hero of *Crime and Punishment*—in a cubbyhole beside the kitchen.

On the day of my arrival Boris invited me to tea in the largest room of the *kommunalnaya*. Our neighbours were assembled on mismatched chairs around a samovar, with a few bottles thrown in for good measure. As we chatted through a somnolent afternoon I watched a plump cockroach crawl along the wainscotting, following the route its ancestors had taken for the past hundred years. It seemed improbable that the sleepy lethargy of this building had ever been seriously disturbed by war or revolution. It was as though the fusty rooms and their occupants were locked in a state of suspended animation, waiting for some cataclysm to rip through the torpid pace of provincial life.

Nepmen of the Nineties

The new Russia is controlled by those who had privilege and power in the old regime. Communism produced its own aristocracy of Party bosses and managers of state enterprises. With their comfortable apartments, luxury dachas, cars, access to special shops, hospitals and schools, the *nomenklatura* were a caste apart from the rest of the population. But they only had rights of use, not ownership. They could be stripped of their privileges if they did not obey their superiors.

The Party ensured its political survival by allowing the masses to glean crumbs from the table. The Soviet state was a vast pool of resources to be pilfered by its citizens. After Stalin's death these sops played a more important role than terror in the maintenance of political stability.

As far back as the Brezhnev era, the *nomenklatura* began to rumble with discontent. They wanted more. Some started to make money in the unofficial economy by syphoning off goods from state enterprises and selling them on the black market. This process accelerated until it gained official sanction as perestroika.

As soon as perestroika allowed them to set up in official business, members of the *nomenklatura* became co-owners of factories, banks, and enterprises. In 1987 party district committees established Centres for Youth Scientific and Technical Creativity with high-ranking *Komsomol* officials in charge.

Members of these Centres took control over profitable new enterprises, concentrating on banking, insurance, international tourism, computer and video sales.

By the 1991 coup, half of all state property had been handed over to companies set up by the *nomenklatura*. Goods disappeared from state shops so rapidly that rationing had to be introduced. The majority of the population resented the fall in their living standards, but there was little they could do to stop the elite from plundering the state.

The new business world attracts ambitious youth. Some young men, and a very few women, have seized the opportunity to claw their way up from the bottom of the pile. These modern *biznesmeni* liken themselves to the old *NEPmen* of the twenties: speculators who profit from scarcity.

My neighbour Boris was one of the few Samarans who seemed excited by his changing world. Like other local parvenus, he adopted what he believed were the trappings of a successful Western businessman. Cultural isolation had given him a warped concept of entrepreneurial style. The biro in his breast pocket had *BISNES* stamped on it in Roman script. Whenever I heard the strains of some Rod Stewart song in the corridor of Specialist Alley I would know that Boris had just returned from his latest business deal. He carried a ghetto blaster with him everywhere, in faithful imitation, he assured me, of an English aristocrat.

A working class boy without connections, Boris had been brought up surrounded by drunkenness and misery. He escaped the brutality of his surroundings by burying himself in books. A hundred years ago poor young men who read books became revolutionaries, and like his forefathers, Boris read to convince himself that there could be a better life than the one he knew. Unlike them, however, he saw his future in terms of private enterprise. Perestroika gave him the chance to put his plans into practice.

"I grew up in a children's home. Mother had to leave her job as a trapeze artiste in the Leningrad State Circus when she got pregnant with me. We came back to Samara to live. My father was a drunkard. Mother left him and found work in a missile factory, but had to live in a women's hostel and wasn't allowed to keep me with her. It was the law of the jungle in the home and you could trust no one. I had no real friends. We were always hungry. The workers in the home were paid next to nothing; they survived by filching food meant for the children. The worst offenders were the director and the chief accountant. They intercepted food the government allocated to the home and sold it. I did not understand this at the time of course, but later I made a point of investigating the system which deprived me. Even then, it was better for me than for the others as I had a mother who came to visit me on Sundays. There was someone in the world who cared about me.

"Every morning at six we were awakened by loudspeakers playing the national anthem. We had to wash, make our beds, have breakfast and go to lessons. All I learned was that it does not pay to be honest. I thought about my mother: she is utterly guileless, and all her life she has been a slave to the state.

"At school the other children mocked me. In those days it was considered shameful to be a 'fatherless child.' They used to put a black line through the space for 'father' on your birth certificate. This practice ended in the mid sixties, but it took a while for the stigma to disappear.

"When I was ten the government finally allocated us a room in a communal flat. We lived way out in an industrial suburb where they make missiles. Even other residents of this city needed special passes to enter our area. I remember hearing explosions from the direction of the factories. Sometimes our house would shake. But everything was hushed up. You never read about what had happened, you just watched the cemeteries fill with graves of those killed in building accidents, chemical and gas explosions. The Chernobyl accident was no surprise to us. Unfortunately for our government that particular radioactive cloud floated off to the West. That's why there was such a fuss."

Boris took me out to the area where he had grown up. Their old wooden house had been pulled down. His mother had been allocated a one-room flat in a *Khrushchev* block. These were built on a more human scale than the ubiquitous twelve-storey concrete slabs that have been erected since the seventies.

The flat was flooded with sunshine. Its balcony overlooked a grassy yard where *babushki* sat on benches under trees. Children tormented each other under watchful eyes. Beds of hollyhocks and sweet william framed entranceways. A man stood in the yard surrounded by a crowd of urchins. A hawk was perched on his arm, attached by a chain to his wrist.

"This part of Russia has been famous since the middle ages for its falconers," said Boris. "When people move from the country into the city they bring their birds with them to keep in their flats. Sometimes they take them out to the countryside to hunt.

"It looks peaceful out there but in fact this area is full of alcoholics, junkies, and criminals. Last Sunday they took away a drunk woman from our stairway who had been beaten half to death. The neighbours heard her screaming but of course no one opened their doors."

A pall of deathly boredom hung over the suburb. We walked a few blocks down to the local supermarket, which was stocked only with bread and stale sweets. Outside a country-woman was selling thick cream from a metal bucket. I produced the litre jar which by now I remembered to take everywhere in case I found something worth buying. Instantly a swarm of little girls gathered, open-mouthed at seeing someone buy so much.

"God, Boris, what was it like to grow up here?"

"The library is the only interesting place in this neighborhood. I used to go there after school so I could read in peace in the empty rooms. I learned about past times and other countries. I realised that the world does not begin and end in this deathly place. But I had to walk home by a circuitous route. If the local lads saw me with books they would accuse me of fancying myself and beat me up."

At dusk we waited to take a bus back to the city centre. Cars came screaming down the main road and pulled to a halt by a vodka shack. A host of unsteady figures emerged from under the trees, shambling in the same direction. When the bus arrived it was full of home-going factory workers with bottles poking out of their pockets. A few were already drunk. I wedged in between their vodka breaths. Boris eyed them in disgust:

"Yes, their lives are hell, but whose isn't? They have no aspirations; they dream no further than the next bottle. How easy they make things for our government. The ideal Soviet man was interested in sport, girls and booze. It's not hard to exploit people like that.

"I decided I wasn't going to go to work in a factory. After leaving school I went to study at the Institute of Culture, and then I began work as a librarian. That depressed me. Readers stole the books and sold them for vodka. Well, it's true I sold books as well, but that was so Mother and I could eat. I would like to lead an honest life, but this system does not allow it. Everyone is corrupt.

"Perestroika enabled me to set up my own business. Some of the first private enterprises to be allowed were public toilets that charged admission. You have seen the cesspit in our central bus station? Well, the first entrepreneurs in our country realised that people would pay for cleaner toilets. One day I found myself stuck in the bus station at Cheboksari in the Chuvash region, where the people are exceptionally stupid. I had an idea. The following week I returned to that bus station and asked for an interview with the manager.

"Now, I am no amateur when it comes to giving bribes. I put forward my proposal and as I rose to leave I let an expensive watch slip off my wrist onto the chair. If the manager had returned it the next day I would have known the deal was off. As it happened he let me organise the toilets.

"I employed the filthiest lush of a *babushka* I could find as an attendant. I knew she would make no effort to keep the place clean, giving me an excuse to sack her without pay. And so every fortnight I would return and kick out whichever old sot I had hired. People still had to pay for the toilets as there was nowhere else for them to go.

"Of course this enterprise could not last forever, and it was a long way to go to collect my earnings. By chance I hit on a business venture nearer home. One day I happened to share a taxi with a Vietnamese man called Han, who was employed in a Toliatti car plant. In the eighties a lot of Vietnamese came over to work in our factories. Even our miserable wages are better than theirs. He told me that Vietnam needed antibiotics. Would I be in a position to help?

"I invented my own pharmaceutical supply company right there on the spot. I told Han he had found the right person, took his order and arranged to meet up the following week.

"I used to work for a pharmacy, typing out orders in the evenings after college. Through this job I got to know two doctors at the city's tuberculosis clinic. Everyone knows that clinic is for dregs, criminals who contract T.B. in gaol. But those doctors were barbarians, alcoholics who didn't give a damn about their patients. They would sit in their surgery swigging vodka and pissing in the sink. They were quite happy to sell me drugs.

"Well, my business expanded until I needed more drugs than the T.B. clinic could supply. I went through the city phone directory listing chemists. Then I called some teenage boys of my acquaintance and sent them all over town to buy penicillin. They chatted up the bored young shop-assistants and got what they wanted without prescriptions. Those chemists who refused to sell were punished. My lads would dump empty pill cartons in their doorways at night. In the morning the chemists would be greeted by a queue of angry customers. If they had been told, as they always were, that there was a shortage of penicillin, what was that pile of boxes doing there?

"Let's say a box of pills cost six roubles; I would give the boys two, and then sell it to the Vietnamese for twelve. In the first fortnight I made as much as my former college tutor earned in a year. More Vietnamese came to me ordering drugs. My lads trawled this whole region; they covered an area larger than Great Britain.

"Eventually prices went up; the business was no longer profitable and the Vietnamese went home. I decided to invest my profits in electronic goods, for it is stupid to hold onto roubles. Through a friend I was accepted into a joint-stock company—one of those private shops you see everywhere."

One Saturday I visited Boris in his little shop in the basement of a crumbling 19th century merchant's mansion. Boris's commercial empire consisted of two counters displaying watches and hand-held electric-shock machines, a pile of pirated American videos in the corner, and a bank of TV sets and video-players behind him. A pornographic film flickered on a screen.

"People are asking for guns all the time but there's a bit of a shortage at the moment, that's why I do a good trade in the zappers."

Many Russians are alarmed by the rise of violent crime, but I could not see the logic in everyone arming themselves to the teeth. One evening Boris had caught me on my way out to the public phone at the end of Specialist Alley. He good-naturedly offered to lend me his gun. I was more scared of it than anything that might be lurking outside. If you are not involved with organised crime here, most trouble comes from drunks. They are a nuisance but not a reason to carry a gun. Boris also had syringes on display. A group of scruffy kids came in and bought a handful. "Junkies!" Boris called after them in delight.

"This is a profitable business, for the time being. If the government changes we could be shut down overnight. This is pure speculation. It's the only way to make money. Why do I want money? To buy people of course. You can't buy a dog with it, it wouldn't understand. But people do, and the bigger the bureaucrat, the more expensive he is."

Boris's girlfriend worked on the other counter of the shop, presiding over a counter of French perfume and after-shave; behind her hung a display of imported polyester frocks. She and Boris paid 15% of their sales to the owners of the shop.

Some of the stock had been brought down from Moscow to be sold at a 50% mark-up; some of it was booty brought in by returning package-tourists from Turkey and The Emirates. Boris also had connections with Samara's small population of African and Middle Eastern medical students. These came from countries friendly to the former USSR. In order to support themselves they brought in goods from home, such as leather jackets, which they sold to speculators like Boris. He was always willing to relieve them of their dollars and foreign clothing.

The director of the shop was an elegant woman who in Soviet times had been a chief engineer in a ball-bearing factory. Raisa Stepanova and her husband had raised the money to open their shop in the usual way, by selling off state property on the black market. As part of the technological elite they had good connections. The third director of the shop was a retired KGB colonel who had been able to bulldoze through the necessary paperwork. Raisa said her biggest hurdle had been a psychological one—speculation was a serious crime in the old Soviet Union. At first she could not bring herself to tell her old friends what she was doing. Now she laughs and says, "I am a *spekulant*, pure and simple. I buy goods for a lower price and sell them for a higher one. I am making money that I never could have dreamed of in the past. We have just managed to buy a separate flat for my mother-in-law, so at last we have a home to ourselves. We have also bought a public bath-house which has to be renovated before we can open it. It's a nightmare. Every day the foreman phones to ask for the workmen's wages. They drank their first week's pay and did no work. Now they are refusing to do any more until they are paid. You see how our Russian system works."

Anyone who wants to start a business in Russia needs protection against competitors and extortionists. Boris had a local mafia chief, a former KGB man, who took care of him. Last year a gang of local hoodlums had decided they wanted a share of Boris's profits. They lay in wait for him outside his mother's flat. Boris went to his protector who sent his goons along to deal with them. I asked Boris what he did in return.

"Oh we go back a long way. He knows I am good at forging documents. I help him in that respect. I even forged my own workbooks. You know that every citizen has to have a record of where they have worked, for how long, and their attitude and conduct. In one of my books it is noted that I have a higher education, in another it is not. It's useful to be flexible. So you see, there is a way around everything in our system."

Boris is destined to remain small-fry. He found himself thwarted when he tried to move into bigger business. He wanted to open a pizzeria, a good idea in this city devoid of safe eating places. Apart from one or two workers' canteens, city restaurants are mafia watering holes. Boris paid 500 US dollars to a local government official to ease the paperwork. The bribe having been paid, the bureaucrat told Boris he would have to wait two years before anything could be done. Shortly afterwards the bureaucrat's son was seen driving a new car. Boris fulminated for a long time, but could do nothing. Not even his mafia boss could help him on that level.

"That bureaucrat is like a pilot fish," he said, "Safe in the shadow of the shark who was placed in office by Yeltsin himself."

The mafia is a mysterious body. No one could or would cite names, although it is generally known that its chiefs are former members of the *nomenklatura* and the KGB. The smaller mafiosi—drivers, bodyguards and enforcers—are highly visible in their foreign cars, gold jewellery and shell-suits. They left their calling cards all over town; almost every week I would pass a newly burned-out roadside kiosk.

The mafia's female consorts tottered around the shops in stilettoes and furs. I used to see these ladies in the central market picking out pineapples that cost a school teacher's weekly wage. Exceptions among Russian women, they did not work. In the past it was usual even for wives of Party bosses to have jobs. Now the mafia wife is free to spend her days shopping for clothes in a hard currency store and taking aerobics classes.

One day Boris introduced me to a wild-eyed man in his late thirties. "This is Volodya, an old friend of mine." Flashing an identity card, Volodya said, "I bet you haven't seen one of these before. It's the most fearsome kind—KGB. I used to be an officer in our Committee for State Security. Now I work in a new commercial bank as head of security.

"When the bank started business it lost so much through bad debts that it decided to form this security department. Three other former members of the KGB work under my direction. Although it costs over 2,000 dollars a month in wages alone the bank has found it pays off. We brought with us a lot of information about the city's inhabitants and have built up a computer data bank on would-be borrowers. Even so, we have to go out almost every night to chase up bad debts.

"When our creditors fail to pay they are given an evening visit. Two members of the security department ride out with two enforcers, usually former sportsmen. We indicate the debtor's flat, and remain in the car so our faces are not seen. The sportsmen knock and sometimes the mere sight of them is enough to induce the debtors to pay up.

"Today a client came into the bank clutching his ribs (they never leave marks on the face). He owed us 16,000 dollars. He said, 'Congratulations, you have a very efficient security service. Let me warn you that if they beat me up again I'll go to the police.' We looked suitably amazed and asked what he was talking about."

I interjected that it is all very well beating people up but it may not actually bring the money back. Was the bank not empowered to seize their goods and chattels?

"Right now we have a lorry loaded with walnuts parked in the forecourt of the bank. Its Armenian owner could not pay back his credit. We often seize cars, but you can be sure if someone is doing a disappearing act they clean out their apartment first. Besides that, we cannot take a flat that has children living in it. I'll give you an example: two men and a woman started a company by paying 10,000 roubles each for the registration papers. The woman showed us these documents and gave the name of another firm as a guarantor. We failed to check this reference but lent the woman four million roubles. When she failed to pay the debt we went to the guarantors who denied all knowledge of the woman. So we beat up the two other partners in the company until they told us where she lived. There we found a flat with six children under 14 living in it. None of them knew where she was. She may be in Vladivostock by now. We returned to her partners.

"We have ways of persuading people to co-operate. A colleague of mine has just bought the city's old mortuary. It has a well in the courtyard. No one knows how deep it is. If you pitch a stone in you never hear a splash. The mere threat of being suspended down this well is usually enough.

"The woman's partners came to see me in the bank. They congratulated us on the efficiency of our security service and told us not to bother to call again, they would look for the woman themselves. By this we understood they would go to the Toliatti mafia. For a high enough sum, or 45% of the money recovered, these people will find anyone from our region anywhere in the world. The bank is insured against bad debts. At first our insurance company refused to pay against a claim, so we sent bandits working for another insurance company to beat up the director of the first company. He paid up.

"My job at the bank is better-paid than with the KGB, but less secure. Everyone knows what I do now, even though we try to keep our faces hidden. I would feel happier about my daughter's future if we could emigrate."

Volodya invited Boris and me to dinner one evening, to meet his wife and daughter. Accepting out of curiosity, I was surprised to find they lived in a far-off, insalubrious *micro-raion*. Their concrete block was indistinguishable from hundreds of others. Their flat had the standard two rooms, kitchen, bathroom and balcony. Perhaps they had more cut-glass on their shelves than usual, but I had expected a higher standard of living. The flat had double front doors, the outer one made of metal. Russians with anything worth stealing now advertise the fact this way.

Volodya and his wife had just returned from the christening of their daughter. He radiated cheerful cruelty, cracking jokes about midnight visits, "Like the thirties. Today a man came in and assured us that when he received the money owed to him the bank would be second in line for repayment. I asked why we would only be second. 'Because the others did a better job of beating me up than your boys.'"

Volodya said that he had done his KGB training in Georgia. When Mrs. Thatcher visited on her tour of the former USSR he had been assigned to shadow her in a Tblisi theatre.

"A dapper man approached me: 'KGB I presume?' he asked."

Volodya roared with laughter at his memory of the MI6 man, "just like Sherlock Holmes." After dinner he leaned his arms on the table and fixed his pale eyes on me: "I am fed up with Russia. There is no future for my family here. Do you think there might be a job for me advising your security forces?" I disappointed him with the truth that I had no contacts in that field. I was sure he had not been the first to offer, and MI6 probably already knew all they needed to know.

On the way home I started to laugh at the absurdity of our meeting, but Boris was in a huff, vexed over my reply to Volodya. The Asiatic mode of personal relations demands that one promises everything to those one wants to impress. Refusals are signals that a bribe is expected.

The money economy has never reigned supreme in Russia. Even before the revolution the writer Alexei Nikolayevich Tolstoy said that in St. Petersburg everyone depended for something on someone else. Mental score cards of favours granted and received formed the foundation of the social system. The rule of *blat* (a system of influence and connections) became the mechanism by which the Soviet system ran. It produced a society in which objective truth has little significance. Samarans suffer no guilt over lying through expediency, but they worry deeply about saying the wrong thing or offending the wrong person.

Pushkin said that his fellow countrymen lied in order to make life more interesting. They preferred cheerful falsehoods to the naked truth. I believe that nowadays their apparent mendacity arises more from need than frivolity. They regard truth as a matter of orthodoxy or heresy rather than an absolute. In the past, adherence to this truth—whether a Tsarist decree or the Party line—meant the difference between life and death.

The chameleon nature of Russian thought stems from this desire to give the right impression at all costs. Boris believed in whichever version of reality it was advisable to believe in. The next day he could tell an opposite story with equal, and genuine conviction. Most Samarans had this facility—it was part of their survival kit.

At first my prosaic Western mind struggled to clutch at solid facts which would then dissolve and float away from my grasp. I floundered amongst the lies and promises, believing that my survival depended on retaining my own conception of the truth. I often had to remind Boris that I wanted his true opinion, and not the version he thought I would like to hear.

Finally I decided to relax my Western belief in the sanctity of objective truth and savour the fluidity of Russian thought. Those around me were unconcerned if two and two made five, for there was no policeman in their heads telling them that to lie is to sin.

The Wise-Woman

"And since man is unable to carry on without a miracle he will create miracles of his own, and will worship the miracle of the witch-doctor and the sorcery of the wise-woman." DOSTOEVSKY: The Grand Inquisitor in *The Brothers Karamazov*

Lina Ivanovna Shatalova was our local wise-woman. She lived in a tiny hut in the courtyard that led off Specialist Alley. Her foetid hovel was crammed with chickens, rabbits, and stray dogs and cats that she had rescued from the streets. She lived without running water and her only heat came from an old gas stove. A little silver haired woman, Lina constantly darted about the hut as she talked, pulling kittens from their perches on the stove and rearranging them on the window ledge. Every so often she would stop to ask me a question, her eyes trans-fixing me over the top of her Trotsky spectacles. I came to value her as the wisest and most broad-minded of my friends in the city. We were both outsiders. Born in the Ukraine, Lina was conscious of a world beyond Samara. Her hut became the hub of my social life. With her alleged powers of healing and second sight, Lina was an influential figure in her neighbour-hood. From morning till late at night people came to her for herbal concoctions, massages or card readings.

"If someone brings me a photo of a relative I can tell what their illnesses are or whether they will go to gaol. I read futures in the cards, but I never accept money for this.

"I know remedies for most diseases. For all forms of cancer, for example, take three fly agaric mushrooms with their roots and soak each one in 90 degree proof spirit. Wrap the jars in a black cloth and stand in the window for nine days. Drink 50 grammes of the liquid three times a day."

Lina's cronies represented a hotchpotch of nationalities from the surrounding streets. Zhenya was a raddled old Gypsy from Moldova who would sit by the gate to the yard, seizing passers-by and almost forcing them to cross her palm with silver. When she heard my accent she laughed so hard I feared her massive bosoms would burst out of their lurex casing. Fascinated by my tape recorder, she leaned her greasy head on my shoulder and cackled as I played back her voice. Lina said Zhenya's family had made a fortune by buying up drinking chocolate in Samara and selling it back in Moldova for three times the price.

Vera the Cossack looked like an ageing drag queen with her vivid red hair, turquoise eye-shadow, exaggerated magenta lips and fistfuls of gold rings. She graciously sat herself on Lina's most comfortable stool and held forth about the meanness of Russians in comparison to her compatriots from Rostov-on-Don.

"My neighbour denounced me for selling vodka without a licence. Well, it's true I was selling vodka, but what can I do, with an invalid son to support?"

"Who is in gaol for GBH," whispered Lina Ivanovna.

With great relish Vera then related the agonizing and untimely death of her daughter-in-law from cancer. She glanced over at a teenage boy who was having his chest massaged by

Lina Ivanovna and silently mouthed the word 'womb,' in the way of genteel women the world over.

One day I called to find a tall pregnant girl sitting in a corner of the hut. Unusually, she did not react to my foreignness, but seemed to be in a dream of her own. Any slight movement from Lina's menagerie made her jump.

"Come back after two o'clock," said Lina, "I can't do a reading while a church service is being held. It won't work." The girl stood up unsteadily and left the hut.

"Her husband has been missing for five days," Lina explained. "Yesterday I had a dream about him. He cried out to me that he was freezing cold. I am sure he is dead. I'm afraid he got himself involved with the mafia through his weakness for women, drink and gambling. Last week my son saw him by the market with a woman in his car who was obviously mafia bait. I've known him for twenty years. He is not a bad lad but he's too attracted to money. He thought he could get rich quickly."

An emaciated kitten laid itself out on the floor and shuddered. Lina threw a cloth over it. "That one has the plague." She saw the look on my face. "Don't worry, humans can't catch it. I had all the other animals innoculated but I couldn't get that little one in time."

A week later I called in at the hut. Lina had just returned from the funeral of the missing man.

"They found him with his hands and tongue cut off and his eyes gouged out. He owed 4,000 dollars to the mafia. I told his wife to go into hiding."

Over the weeks Lina related the story of her life.

"I lived like tumble weed, blowing around the USSR. There is nothing exceptional about this; it has been the fate of many of my generation.

"I was born in 1934, just after the Ukraine's great famine, a result of collectivisation. My mother was malnourished while she was carrying me and I was born prematurely. I have always been small for my age. My mother did not care for me very much; she used to say I was an old lady in a child's body.

"I was seven when the war began, and conscious of what it is to be a human being on this earth. My first impression of the war was not frightening. We lived in Proskurov, a village in the Western Ukraine, on the main road to Russia. It was near the town of Vinnitsa, where Hitler made his headquarters.

"In every country people act the same way—they toady after whoever is in power. Those villagers whom the Soviet authorities had dispossessed as *kulaks* welcomed the invaders. As the Germans swept past our house on motorcycles the former *kulaks* came out offering bread and salt. Later some of these men were killed by the partisans. Anyone who had held Communist Party positions tried very hard to conceal the fact. Some just quietly left the village.

"The Soviet army retreated before the German advance. This was the worst part of the war. There were a lot of deserters because soldiers feared they would be shot by the Soviet authorities if they went back east, but of course they did not want to fall into German hands, so they stayed around our part of the country. Some married Ukrainian women. Others changed their surnames. They burned their documents and learned Ukrainian. They tried to forget their own language. They did all this just to remain alive. After all, life is the dearest thing to us.

"At the beginning of the occupation there was little violence in our town. I think there is more here today among our native Russians than there was at that time. When the partisans started to operate, then of course things grew bloody.

THE WISE-WOMAN

29

"Jews were not shot in front of the villagers, but rounded up and sent off to camps. Many escaped into the countryside where they were hidden by villagers. Gypsies too, they changed their costumes to look like Ukrainians. I saw many Jews and Gypsies return to our village after the war.

"We had Germans living with us in the largest room of our house. One of them, Karl, was a kind and intelligent man. He used to say, 'Hitler is wrong, he will lose. He is pushing his armies too far. They will die of the Russian cold like Napoleon's army.' I think Karl was some sort of anti-fascist. He lived with us for two years, but was eventually shot by the partisans.

"The Germans were cunning—they got others to work for them. Many village children of 16 or 17 went off to labour camps in Germany. They were usually the sons and daughters of dispossessed kulaks. I remember how bitterly the women cried as they saw their children off. Some were never seen again.

"After the war girls started to return from Germany to our village. Most were either pregnant or had babies. No one would marry them. I know some of their children. In later years they came to me in Novokuibyshevsk, which is not far from here. I helped set them on their feet and they found some sort of happiness. They were outcasts back in the Ukraine. No one wanted anything to do with the 'German parcels.'

"In the 1960s I went back to Proskurov for a visit. I heard that the postmistress, a girl of 22, had died in another town. She died of cancer of the womb. She had no relations with men; she simply did not function as a woman. But she lived her whole life as the butt of insults for being a 'German parcel.' She led such an unhappy life in our village that she left home, developed cancer and died.

"In the spring of 1944 Russian forces reached our village. The Germans were taken by surprise and fled across the Southern Bug river. Then they retaliated, holding the Russians back for two weeks.

"There was a German post near our house. The soldiers were gathered together drinking schnapps when they heard the first Russian tank approach. We children were watching out of the window. The Germans ran away half-naked, dressed only in their nightshirts and wooden slippers. We laughed at them.

"Our house lay between the main road and the river so we got caught up in the battle. Six Russian tanks rolled along the highway and one turned off into our yard, halting between the barn and the well.

"We were all huddled together in the kitchen, behind sandbags. Mother was praying to herself: 'Thank God, thank God, our troops are here. They'll liberate us.'

"We heard the tank fire at the Germans on the other side of the river. As it fired it recoiled and crashed backwards through our kitchen wall. Then it drove forwards again, leaving a great hole and a pile of rubble. As the smoke and dust settled we could see the battle raging through the hole in the wall. You can imagine how frightening that was!

"Suddenly a German stumbled in through the wall. He had been shot in the leg and three of his fingers were broken. They flapped loosely from his hand. He cried, 'I'm not German, but Swiss. I was taken prisoner by the Germans. The officers made me fight against my will.' Mother was scared. What if the Russians came and found him sheltering with us? '*Pan,* go over there to the German post,' she told him. Mother wanted to take him across to it but the fighting prevented them from moving.

"After a few hours the shooting and shelling came to a halt. The Russian army had reached our street. We caught sight of a Soviet officer standing outside our house. My mother she rushed outside to him. 'Comrade, we have a German with us. He has given himself up as a prisoner.'

"The officer was a tiny man but very high ranking. He brought two soldiers with him, armed with sub-machine guns. They came in through the front door and halted beneath our icons, facing the German. He repeated his story: 'I am Swiss, a prisoner of the Germans. I did not want to fight against Stalin.' The officer pointed to the man's leg and asked, 'What's that then? Who gave you that wound?' And before he could answer the officer took out his pistol and shot him through the neck.

"We children had hidden ourselves behind the stove and saw everything. It's not true the way films show someone shot, 'Bang! Bang!' and they fall down dead. It's not that simple at all. You can't imagine what a huge fountain of blood spurts from the throat. The German fell, and his blood went on pumping out. It splattered all over the wall.

"The Russians left, and then a neighbour boy came running for Granny: 'Auntie Nastya! Auntie Nastya! The Germans are coming back!' Granny had to clean the room and get rid of the body because if the Germans came and found it they would have shot us. She ran out to their deserted post and brought back a discarded greatcoat. She washed the bloody wall down with it and threw it into the stove, but it would not burn because it was so wet. Granny had to run out again to fetch some kerosene.

"There was a disused well in our yard. The adults dragged the corpse out and threw it down the well, uniform and all. Then they threw in branches and snow to cover their traces.

"I have often wondered who that German or Swiss man

was. In spring neighbour boys tried to pull up his body from the well. It had vanished without trace.

"I think fear is less terrible for a child than for a grown-up. I was scared by the fighting but I soon grew used to it. Every day after the firing had stopped—and it always stopped at six o'clock—I would step out into the street to sniff the air. War has a unique smell. It smells of burnt wool and baked potatoes and beetroots. An ironic smell! They used to smack me for going out to sniff the air, but I didn't care. I was so attracted by that smell; I can recall it to this day.

"When the Germans finally retreated our house was a ruin. A shell had demolished the living room wall. It crashed in, bringing down clocks and icons. Eight of us had to live in the kitchen, which was the only room left with a roof over it. We all went hungry. Mother was the only able-bodied person in our house. The Germans had forced her to go out digging trenches, and the Russians made her do the same. We had very little left. The Germans had taken anything they fancied, and so had the Russians. Yes, our side stole too. They helped themselves.

"Now in my old age I think about the process of winning and losing power. The Germans ruled us for four years and did not manage to destroy communism, but Gorbachev and Yeltsin got rid of it in an instant. However, we do not yet have capitalism. We don't understand it. All people do is buy and sell. We produce nothing. We only have speculation and the mafia.

"Famine took hold after the war ended. As soon as children's homes started to be organised Mother used her influence as a teacher to have us placed in them. That way she knew we would be fed. Later she came and took my sisters back home, leaving me behind. Years later I asked her why and she replied that she did not know herself. Before Grandad died in 1946 he begged her to bring me home, but it was no good, Mother had the power in our house. But Grandad told me how to survive: 'A loving calf suckles two udders. You must learn to be kind and loving all your life. That way no one will hurt you.'

"In the children's home I fell ill with food poisoning and was sent away to Murmansk by mistake. My name was Davidenko but they had written Davidova on the forms. We also went hungry in Murmansk, but a kind man up there, a sailor, fed us scallops from the Gulf. However I fell ill again from eating tainted cabbage. They sent me off to the mining town of Cheremkhova in Siberia, and from there to Maikop in the Northern Caucasus. No children's home wanted to take me, sick as I was, for if I died it would have looked bad on their records.

"While I lay unconscious in the hospital at Maikop an old man spotted me through the windows. He asked about me and learned that I was not expected to recover and that no relations came to visit me. When he heard this he sent in cheese and skins full of sour milk which I drank through a straw.

"The first time I woke up and saw the old man by my bed I fainted. I thought he was the devil and my heart froze. In Cheremkhova they had told us a story about a fearsome evil creature called the cyclops. I believed the cyclops had come for me.

"The next day the old man brought me a pair of shoes with high heels. It was my first pair of high heels; I was thirteen then. He also gave me his green lizard to play with. It had a little iron collar around its neck and a lead. He fed it flies and let me keep it in the ward near my bed. It used to hang off my fingers by its tail.

"One day the old man came with a hide jacket lined with wool that he had made for me. He wrapped it around my shoulders and took me outside where he had a mule waiting. In one pannier there were loaves of bread; he popped me into the other. At first I crouched in the bottom of the basket, too terrified to move. But as we plodded onwards I peeped out to see where we were going. We were heading towards a range of beautiful far-away mountains. We started to climb up and up through fields of maize. On we went until it seemed as though we would take off and fly up to the very peaks, but we stopped at a strange and frightening house built of great stones. It looked like a wizard's lair.

"Sheep and goats were penned in a corner of the ground floor. Pretty little chicks hopped about. The old man set me down to sleep among the animals. But for the first night I dared not fall asleep, fearing that the man would come in and eat me. In the morning he brought me some sour milk. 'Drink!'

"I drank through fear, but later I realized the milk was to help me get well. He fed me meat and various sorts of berries. Every evening he rubbed grease on my back. I began to grow used to the old man. He was lonely and reserved, but as he went about his work he sang songs in his language. I started to call him 'Atta,' which means father. In our own ways we understood each other.

"He was of the Islamic faith, a Chechen perhaps, or Circassian. He gave me baggy trousers and a scarf to wear. My hair had been cut short in the children's homes, but he wanted me to grow it long. Once a neighbour woman found little insects in my hair. She called him and he came running, crying, 'Oh no, she's fallen ill again!' He was always afraid my sickness would return.

"There was a teacher in the neighbourhood who spoke

Russian. She explained that my Atta's three sons had been killed at the front and their mother had died of grief. He had seen me in the hospital and asked if he could take me away. They were worried that he just wanted a servant, but he said, 'You've given her up for dead. Let me take her.'

"I loved my Atta. He was a very kind man. I had loved my Grandad and I quickly grew used to living with this old man. I told the authorities I wanted him to adopt me, but my mother would not give her consent.

"Eventually, in 1949, I was told I had to go to live with my real father. I screamed and wept and clung to my Atta but they took me away. I wrote to him for a few years after that but we never saw each other again.

"My parents had divorced before the war, when I was very small. Father had remarried and lived on a huge *sovkhoz* near Volgograd. I was very shy with my father's new family. They were well off, and I was not used to rich people. Father was a little ashamed that he had not been around during my childhood and I sensed he wanted to make it up to me. He was always slipping me tasty morsels of food. But all the same I wanted to leave that house.

"The *sovkhoz* employed many refugees, including a Jewish couple who had a workshop where invalids sewed little shirts, trousers and sheets for children's homes and kindergartens. One day I went to have a look at the workshop, hoping they might take me on. The first thing I noticed was a man with no legs sitting on top of a huge billiard table in the middle of the room. He was like a little monkey, propelling himself about the table with his arms. His sharp eyes watched everything around him.

"He told me to sit down and look through a folder of drawings and designs. I felt him studying me. 'Do you really want to sew?' he asked at last. 'Yes, of course.' He sat me at a machine and I began to learn. Granny had already taught me to stitch evenly so I made quick progress. I was left-handed like my teacher, which pleased him.

"My teacher's name was Mikhail Abramovich Ivstaigeri. He was a Jew from the Crimea. He lost his legs in 1914, during the first war. When the second world war broke out the Crimea was cut off and some of the local Tartars began to hand Jews over to the Germans. The Ivstaigeris fled by boat and came as refugees to that *sovkhoz*.

"I studied with them for two years. Mikhail Abramovich would ignore my requests for help as I worked, letting me sew the whole day long. Finally he would come over to scold me, to tell me where I had gone wrong. He was eccentric. He would say to me, 'When you were at the bath house, what did you see?'

'I saw a lady with a very broad back.'

'Now listen, how would you make a dress for such a woman?'

'I would make little tucks to shape it to her back.'

'You are right, and in the front she will have breasts and a big belly. You must sew the dress so that big belly is not visible. Next time you go to the bath-house pay attention to their rumps: fat, small, scrawny . . .'

"Mikhail Abramovich and his wife always spoke to each other courteously in their lovely accent. To tell you the truth, I have never seen that sort of respectful attentiveness among Russian couples. We are a coarse people.

"I was surprised at how miserably the Ivstaigeris lived. I thought that such talented, hard-working people should be rich.

"They were very fond of me. After I left the *sovkhoz* I wrote to them and visited when I could. When Mikhail Abramovich died his wife followed him to the grave two months later; she did not want to go on living without him. I was very upset when they died. Once again friends had left me alone in this life.

"I left the *sovkhoz* in 1950. My sister Galya understood that life was not exactly sweet with my father's family, so she sent for me to come and live with her in the town of Novokuibyshevsk. At that time Galya lived in a girl's hostel. There was room for me there with her, but she had great difficulty in finding me a job. Novokuibyshevsk was a new town under construction on the right bank of the Volga, so there was plenty of building work available. I was 16 but so short and skinny everyone took me for 13. One foreman said, 'She'll soon be covered over with a shovelfull of earth and we'll have to answer for it.'

"In desperation my sister took me to the *Komsomol* district secretary and told him I could not find a job. The secretary, a handsome, good-natured man, said, 'Let her work in a canteen!'

"So I became an apprentice cook in canteen number four. That suited me: it was warm in the kitchen and I was glad to have indoor work. I had no winter boots and there was absolutely no warm clothing available in those days.

"I worked there for 18 months and was always in high spirits, although we were paid almost nothing. We were a jolly brigade. We used to hold concerts in the dining room, all dressed up in freshly laundered caps and overalls. Our instruments were hunks of meat and bones. A femur would make a double bass, two thin bones a violin, and ribs were our accordion. We sang and played on our bones. We ended up filthy and covered in blood but everyone loved our concerts.

"There were frequent explosions in Novokuibyshevsk, in the chemical plants, the gas works . . . a lot of people died during those years. There is a big cemetery where they are buried. You'd hear an explosion—boof! and that was all; it would be hushed up by the authorities. I used to hear the emergency sirens go off in the night and my heart would freeze.

"In 1953 my sister discovered she was pregnant. When her boyfriend heard this he left, telling her he was going on a business trip to Moscow. Galya was employed in an oxygen plant. In those days you worked up to the eighth month of pregnancy and had one month's rest. They did not get such long leave as they do today. It was very heavy work, filling cylinders with oxygen. I worried about her doing this hard and dangerous job.

"One night when my sister was on duty there was an explosion. I heard the sirens go off and leaped out of bed. I ran to the phone and rang and rang. They would tell us nothing, only that there was a blaze somewhere inside the plant. At six o'clock in the morning a car came to the hostel. They told me my sister was in a grave condition and drove me down to the first aid post (we did not even have a hospital then). I looked in the ward but she wasn't there. Then they brought her in on a trolley. The doctor put her arms around me and said, 'Have courage, little daughter.'

"My sister had no eyelashes. Her skin was black. It looked like charcoal. I wept. I screamed, 'Galya! Galya!'

"She looked at me but did not recognise me. They laid her on a bed and hung two big oxygen balloons over her. Thin tubes led into her nostrils. After a while the doctor said, 'Now we shall take off the oxygen mask. Then she'll be able to talk to you. Sit down.'

"The nurse gave her an injection. She opened her eyes and fixed them upon me.

'All your life, all your life, I shall appear before your eyes like this, unless you take care of the baby.'

'What baby?' I asked. Only then did I remember that she had been pregnant. The doctor said that the child had been born alive.

'All your life, all your life, I shall stand before you with the eyes that you see looking at you now, unless you take my baby,' Galya repeated.

"That was all. She was tortured by pain the whole day. Towards evening she opened her eyes for the last time. Then she lost consciousness. I thought she was dozing but she died. I didn't think death would be like that.

"They prepared her for burial as though she were a suckling pig, cleaning and scraping off her burnt black skin.

"Three other people had been killed that night. A spark had set off a gas explosion.

"I was alone, how could I bury her? Well, my workplace helped me. The director of the oxygen plant arranged for cars to take us to the cemetery and back to the canteen. There my workmates had laid out food and vodka.

"I didn't see the baby until two weeks later. She stayed in the maternity home for 15 months and I looked after her on Sundays, my day off. No one else could adopt her as the laws were very strict about that. During this time my sister's lover Vassily Vassilievich Shatalov made enquiries and learned that I had the child. One day he turned up.

'You must be Lina.'

'Yes.'

'Will you marry me?'

"I thought he was joking so I replied:

'Why not? I might as well marry such a fine figure of a man!'

"That was all. We did not discuss it any further. Three days later I returned home from work to find my things had disappeared from the corner of the room where I slept. My friends said, 'That Shatalov came and took your things away. He said you are going to get married.'

'What are you talking about? I'm not going to marry anyone. I never gave him my promise.'

"I had only been joking and he thought I was serious. However Vassily Vassilievich was a very handsome and interesting man. He had a good job as head of the district construction team. I had no reason to refuse him. I lived with his female relatives for two weeks and then we held our wedding. We were advised not to let anyone know that Tania wasn't my child.

"At first Vassily Vassilievich and I lived happily together, but then the differences in our ages and temperaments began to show. He was 11 years older than me and we did not get along very well. He began to insult me, saying I was not good enough for him. Male chauvinism played a large role in his consciousness.

"I took a job as a carriage attendant on the railways—a *provodnitsa*. In Russia this is not considered a very respectable job for a woman, but I loved it. I met all sorts of interesting people. At first Vassily Vassilievich was happy for me to travel up to Moscow and bring back cheap clothes and food. When I did my job so well that they asked me to work as the train's chief attendant, warfare broke out at home. My husband accused me of wanting to run after men. He said he was ashamed to admit that I was his wife. In the end, after 14 years of torment, I left him.

"I lived alone for two years. I was still young and had a lot of admirers. Some of them were good and honourable men, but I was scared of making the same mistake again. I was poor and uneducated. Then I fell in love with Volodya.

"Well, I married Volodya. He was a good man, but weak. One day he slunk off with another woman. She had a hump back, but she was rich. He left me with three children, whom I educated. I was proud and never asked him for money. I supported my family by sewing.

"Now I live alone. I have my 15 cats and the dogs. I get up early to feed the pigeons. Crows sit on the roof and caw until I come out to feed them. One of them broke his wing last year. I mended it and now he brings his family. I thank God every morning and evening that I am alive.

"Next spring I am going to move to the countryside. I have found a little house there. It's in a bad state but no worse than this one. I don't want my children to worry about me. It preys on their conscience to see me living in such misery. Tania asked me to live with her family in Orenburg, but I could not live in a flat in the city. My savings will pay for a decent burial; I need nothing else.

"It suits me to be an old maid. Some women can't live without men, but I am not one of them. Vera once said to me, 'It's true I never wed, but I always had a man in bed.' It's her hobby, shall we say.

"My son also wanted me to marry again. He said, 'Mama, marry while you've still got your looks. After they go no one will want you.'

"I thought about it and decided I did not need another

man, someone to boss me around. You see how our Russian men are—they have no principles in their relation to women. They are not like yours. Over there, couples share responsibilities. Here, the woman has to do everything: housework, paid job, with never a day off. It is simply a life of drudgery. And the man can go out, get drunk and run around with women. That is normal life in Russia.

"Now I live by healing and telling fortunes. I learned everything from my grandmother, whom I loved more than anyone in the world. She made me memorise her spells and remedies. I was not allowed to write anything down. She told me to pay attention to people, saying, 'Not everyone is alike. Some run through their lives and achieve absolutely nothing. They do no good; they are simply stupid. Some are cleverer, some are kinder, and then there are the pitiless criminals who kill a person as lightly as they might slaughter a chicken.'

"My grandmother cured people in our village, although she was a dressmaker by profession. There was no medicine during the years of the German occupation so villagers came to see her. She began to teach me about healing when I was seven. A shepherd came in with erysipelas where he had been gored by a bull. His leg was like rough old wood. Granny called me over, 'Come here and put your hands on his leg. Don't be scared.'

"I noticed the flesh swell between my fingers as though it were pastry dough. I screamed when I took my hands away, for they had swollen up. Granny said, 'That's enough. You will do this three times more and then he will be cured.' She also told me not to be repulsed by illness: 'This is human pain. Never dismiss it. You must sympathise; you must help. If you see someone in pain or near death your heart must weep tears of blood. That way you will always be able to treat people.'

"This shepherd came three more times. I would place my hands on his leg while Granny recited prayers. He recovered and Granny told me, 'You will cure people, but it will drain your energy. You will live in poverty, your strength will fail you.'

"A Gypsy woman later confirmed her words. This woman was a refugee from Bessarabia whom we sheltered for a while during the German occupation. She looked at my hand and said, 'As for this little one, it would have been better if she had never been born. She will have a hard life, but things will be easy for the people around her.'

"During the war women in our village were desperate for news of their husbands at the front. Of course, many never returned. At full moon the women used to go out into a nearby field where a single pine tree stood and where the grass was kept specially mown. The women would take off their gold wedding rings and hold them up till they caught the light of a moonbeam. Then they would look inside the illuminated circle while reciting a prayer.

"One neighbour woman was out in the field when something startled her and she dropped her ring. She searched for it for two weeks but I was the one who found it. Granny told me to take it to the field that night. I looked through that broad gold band and saw a mass of candles and many people. Someone dressed in white walked through the middle of them all. And then I saw a man sitting with a walking stick by his side. That woman's husband returned from the front with one leg amputated. He said they had performed the operation by candlelight as there had been no electricity. The second night I saw a coffin. I saw it very clearly. Shortly afterwards a man came to the owner of that ring and told her that her husband had died of his wounds.

"After that many women came to me wanting to know the fate of their husbands. On moonlit nights Granny would take me out to the field. I had to hold a ring up to the moon, cross my eyes and look through it, saying a prayer about the person I sought:

'Tell me, land where I was born,
Tell me, holder of all secrets,
Is—alive or is he dead?'

"After a long time little sparks would appear, and then a vision. My head would spin and Granny had to stop me from falling.

"One day in 1946 Granny came home from working in the kitchen garden and said, 'Call the family together. I am going to die.'

"I ran to fetch them. Within an hour we had all gathered around the big table in front of the icons. Granny lay on her bed. One by one each member of the family approached and knelt down on her lovely multi-coloured woollen rug. She told each in turn how they should live their lives. Then she said, 'Leave the room. I don't want you to see me die.'

"We sat in the kitchen. We were so many some had to squat on the floor. I closed my eyes and imagined that I was a doctor —I had seen army doctors during the occupation—and that I could save Granny. I must have dozed off. I awoke to darkness and a cry from the room where she lay. No one saw how she died.

"I thought it was the end of the world when Granny died. I wondered how my sisters could play with their dolls. I couldn't touch mine for months."

As I listened to Lina Ivanovna's life story I thought how scarcely communist ideology had penetrated the minds of the poor. Peasant women were workhorses; they saw socialism as just another cross they had to bear. As Lina put it:

"The Germans are a clever and inventive people, but they had fascism, just as we had communism."

The early Bolsheviks may have tried to reach peasant women with propaganda and genuine attempts at social improvement, but when collectivisation was pushed through the majority were even further alienated. A doctor from Lina's home town of Vinnitsa wrote:

"It was easy to proclaim on paper the liberation of women, to promulgate laws which for the peasants of the period had as much meaning as extra-terrestrial signals, and then boast of having established 'socialism.'"[1]

Znakharki, or peasant healers like Lina's grandmother, were anathema to the ideals of Bolshevism, with their mystical and religious beliefs. The new government portrayed the *znakharki* as primitive women, ignorant of hygiene and scientific methods of health care. Doctors' assistants and peasant midwives were trained and sent out to the countryside. This campaign met with resistance from the midwives who were often loathe to return to their peasant roots and from rural women who distrusted "interferers" from the cities.

To effectively undermine belief in peasant healers the Soviet government would have had to provide free, accessible, high quality health care. Civil war, famine, rural chaos during the years of collectivization, and war against Germany made this an impossibility. The *znakharka* tradition never died.

Lina's grandmother's skills were in exceptional demand when civilian health care collapsed during the war. Even during peacetime, prophesying and the casting of "beneficial" spells were tolerated. Lina said that the authorities only prosecuted those who practised black magic. She was not allowed

---

[1] Drs. A. and M. Stern, *Sex and the Soviet Union* (WH Allen, 1981) p. 29.

to advertise her services, but when she went to register herself as a dressmaker (her official profession) the entire finance department in the local government offices, most of them Party members, came over to have their cards read.

Lina Ivanovna had a vast experience of life and human behaviour. In her capacity as agony aunt, matchmaker, soothsayer and doctor, she shrewdly assessed her clients before giving advice. Those who came to see her were usually depressed, naïve and vulnerable, and therefore inclined to believe everything she told them. However she did not tell them what she knew they wanted to hear. The poverty in which she lived showed she was not in the business of extracting money from the gullible. In return for her services Lina accepted presents as signs of appreciation. She tended others through a desire to be loved and needed—she had taken her grandfather's advice to heart.

Those who cannot afford drugs or who doubt their efficacy flock to Lina Ivanovna. Since pharmacies were turned into commercial operations there has been a shortage of drugs throughout Russia. Prices of medicines have soared, imports and domestic output have declined. In 1991 3.4% of Russian GNP was spent on health care. In 1992 this figure was halved.[2]

The mafia have exacerbated the shortage of antibiotics and pain-killers. Doctors at a neighbourhood clinic demanded that they be armed on night duty after a raid on the morphine cabinet by Chechen gangsters. Drug racketeering has tragic consequences. A friend told me that when her cousin was dying of cancer they pleaded with the doctors to give her painkillers. "You supply the drugs, we'll give her the injections," they told her.

---

[2] Russian Labour Review, no. 2, 1993

The pattern of Russian health care is starting to resemble that of some Western countries. The population is supposed to buy medical insurance, but many cannot afford it. Doctors in state hospitals are severely demoralised and most nurses have left the profession because they could not survive on the wages. Female relatives of patients now carry out basic nursing functions on the wards.

Under such circumstances more and more people are turning to the likes of Lina Ivanovna. She herself had a low opinion of doctors:

"So many of them are completely incompetent. Students use *blat* to gain places in prestigious medical schools. Some doctors cannot even understand the Latin names for things!"

The Russian tradition of mixing mysticism with business and politics did not end with the assassination of Rasputin. These days Russia is a paradise for quacks of every description. In the early nineties a "spiritual masseur" called Anatoly Kashpirovsky gained enormous popularity through his televised mass healing sessions. Kashpirovsky was an aide to the ultra-right leader of the Liberal Democratic party, Vladimir Zhirinovsky. Such is the credence given to these charlatans that after the 1993 elections politicians and psychologists met to discuss how Kashpirovsky had manipulated the Russian electorate. Yeltsin promptly passed a law requiring all healers to have a licence.

Fear in the face of change underlies this burgeoning superstition. The Soviet system produced generations accustomed to having their lives arranged for them. Initiative never brought reward. Today Russians find themselves in the unusual position of having to make their own decisions. Unsure of themselves, they consult wise-women for reassurance from beyond. As their world turns upside down, many hope for miracles.

Male Infantilism and Alcoholic Disorder

> *"'Drink will be the ruin of the Russian!' Markelov remarked gloomily.*
> *'It's from grief, Sergei Mikhailovitch,' the coachman said without turning round."*
>
> TURGENEV: *Virgin Soil*

I stood on a bleak suburban station in the early morning drizzle, wondering why the crows had chosen to build their nests on loud speaker platforms rather than trees. As I waited for the local train a few people with hoes and rucksacks gathered on the platform. Boris had warned me of banditry on the Samara-Toliatti line, but my fellow travellers were quiet gardeners off to their allotments. The scene brought back memories of Saturday mornings on the outer reaches of London's Piccadilly line.

The train followed the Volga out through industrial suburbs and past a bend in the river where the rebel Stenka Razin used to ambush cargo boats. Misty water curved around pine-clad hills, rivalling the Rhine at its most picturesque. Half-expecting to find a King Ludwig castle, I alighted instead at a town reminiscent of a post-war British council estate, it's dreariness highlighted by the magnificence of its setting.

A plump middle-aged lady met me at the station. Ludmilla was a friend of Lina Ivanovna's; they had worked together in the Novokuibyshevsk canteen in the sixties. I followed her up a hill between identical brick *Khrushchevi* flats and desolate children's playgrounds. This was another "secret" town; somewhere beneath our feet a huge arsenal was buried.

Ludmilla stopped to show me a newly-opened private shop that was the talk of the town. It displayed a Japanese television set, kiwi fruit liqueur and chocolates which had obviously fallen off the back of a humanitarian aid lorry. The townspeople took a collective pride in these goods which few could afford. Capitalism had not yet taught them that a product acquires true value when it is in your hands and not your neighbour's.

Ludmilla lived with her husband and grandson in a two-room flat. She had papered it in puffy vinyl material, slimy and unpleasant to the touch. She bounced around preparing lunch, jolly as a Girl Guide leader at camp. The food was a mere dressing for the bottles of beer, liqueurs and vodka amassed on the table. Suddenly a little boy rushed through the flat, shouting, "Grandad's here! He's drunk again!"

A little weather-beaten man with a charming smile lurched in. "You must excuse me, I've just flown down from the North. We're laying pipe lines up there. It takes a while to adapt."

"Let's drink to your adaptation," Ludmilla smiled indulgently at her husband.

A couple of neighbours called, also inebriated. They had come from a funeral which was being held in the flat next door. A young man had smashed up his car while drunk. His coffin now stood outside on the landing, adorned with crêpe paper flowers.

We all sat down at the table and the familiar ritual began with a few toasts designed to lift the revellers to a peak of merriment. When conversation became too much effort, they danced. When they tired, they downed more toasts until they collapsed.

One of the company was a huge Cossack who had fought in Afghanistan. Although both his legs had been shattered in the war, he failed to qualify for an invalidity pension because he had only been a regular soldier and not an officer. To support his family he ran a little vodka kiosk. He was wary of me at first, especially as I refused the dried saltfish which is a standard Russian drinking accompaniment.

"What is she, a bourgeois?"

"No, she's a journalist," replied Ludmilla.

Hearing this, the Cossack went off to fetch his photo album. Tears ran down his cheeks as he showed me his fallen comrades. Brusquely, his wife snatched the album from his hands and hurled herself around the room to the beat of a manic pop tune. She pulled her husband up and then the others, until they were all stomping in a frenzied circle. Every few minutes the tipsy Girl Guide whooped with glee.

Embarrassed at having to pretend I was having a good time, I slunk away to the other room. When the noisy revelry subsided I ventured out again. The men lay unconscious on the floor. I sat in the kitchen with Ludmilla as she reminisced about the lost world of her youth.

"I was in the *Komsomol*. We used to organise hikes through the hills. Life was gayer in those days; there was less crime, less greed. I don't know what is happening in our country now. If people would only put their backs into it and work, things would be better. I have always worked; it's the only thing I know how to do. But the younger generation do not believe in anything. My own son is a good-for-nothing. He and his wife spend all their pay on drink. That is why their child lives with me."

At seven in the morning I awoke to the sound of animated

voices. A bottle of vodka had been cracked open in the kitchen. I made my excuses and prepared to leave. Ludmilla's husband gallantly escorted me to the station. I felt conscious of being a wet blanket, but the enthusiasm of these kind people was as alien to me as that of my former school mates on sports day.

As I rode back into Samara on that rainy Sunday morning I pictured its blocks of flats stripped of their façades. In each identical kitchen a man in a white vest would be sitting slumped at a formica table, chasing away his hangover with a fresh bottle and a couple of pickled cucumbers.

Ludmilla's family celebrated their day off in the manner of millions of Russians—by drinking themselves into oblivion. Drinking is their main recreational activity and a precious compensation for life. It is the mechanism of social interaction; to refuse a drink is an insult to one's host. Teetotallers are regarded with extreme suspicion. Non-drinking is a sign of being a loner—an unhealthy trait in Russian eyes. As in many other societies, prodigious drinking is associated with manliness. In reality it masks repression and social ineptness, especially with women. The peasant rebel leader Stenka Razin is said to have thrown his new bride into the Volga when his former drinking partners complained he had deserted them.

Much has been said about Russian drinking habits. In the 17th century a Croatian priest wrote, "What can be said of our drunkenness? If you were to search the whole world over, nowhere could you find such a vile, repulsive and terrible drunkenness as exists here in Russia."[3]

The priest was sent to Siberia for his remarks, but his words

---

[3] Quoted in B. Segal: *Russian Drinking: use and abuse of alcohol in pre-revolutionary Russia* (Rutgers Centre of Alcohol Studies, 1987)

hold true even today. In all my world travels I have never seen such determined self-obliteration through alcohol.

Nineteenth century European travellers in Russia commented upon the comatose figures lying outside every inn, sleeping off the effects of vodka. These days there are fewer restaurants and hotels than in Tsarist times, so the sleeping bodies are distributed all over town, in bus shelters, entranceways and courtyards. As a woman friend wryly observed, "You have a lot of pubs, and we have a lot of streets."

Drunks congregate at railway stations, private kiosks that line the main street, and little beer stands called *pivnushki*. There was a *pivnushka* at the end of Specialist Alley which attracted a constant stream of shabby figures clutching three-litre pickle jars. Once they had filled these they would huddle together to empty the contents. In cold weather, this activity often took place in the entranceway to our tenement. I used to watch these figures leaving the *pivnushka*, fearing they would never make it across the road. Swaying dangerously at the kerbside, they stared ahead with the glazed eyes of mad fish. Sometimes an unsteady couple would link hands and tenderly help each other across the tram tracks.

Some people prefer cheaper and stronger intoxicants such as furniture polish and window cleaner. The department stores are full of *babushki* blowing their pensions on perfumes; in the evening they display their little bottles on upturned crates in the streets. The favourite brand amongst connoisseurs is cucumber face lotion—drunk neat.

In 1986 the militia had to be called to quell a threatened riot in the city's largest store. Staff had limited sales of eau de Cologne to two bottles per customer.[4]

---

[4] Wilson and Bachkatov: *Living with Glasnost* (Penguin, 1988) pp. 151-2.

MALE INFANTILISM AND ALCOHOLIC DISORDER

Alcoholism exacerbates economic chaos beyond measure. Delivery-men are too drunk to carry bread into bakeries, professors cancel classes, and repair men will not lift a finger until they are given a bottle. I sometimes faced shop assistants too paralytic to serve. A medical student told me he had watched surgeons perform operations with shaking hands.

Although women drunks are less visible than their male counterparts, female alcoholism is high by Western standards. Women usually drink at home or at work rather than on the street. Most Western commentators on Russia are men and therefore unlikely to witness the enthusiastic drinking that takes place amongst women. Women tend to be more restrained in mixed company. When they feel free from the need to keep an eye on their menfolk they throw themselves into drinking and dancing as a release from the stress of everyday life. Watching a group of dignified university lecturers kick up their heels, it wasn't hard to imagine their peasant forebears dancing and downing vodka at harvest time.

Yet drinking must be less damaging to general female health than the perpetual infantilism they nurture in their men. Female care allows men to make an art form of irresponsibility. They learn to cope with life with a bottle in the hand and a woman in the kitchen.

I wondered whether these men might learn to look after themselves if women were to refuse to pick up the pieces. My female acquaintances thought this question as foolish as if I had suggested a new-born baby be left to feed itself. They did not subscribe to the Western concept of individual responsibility, especially where men were concerned. I believe they fostered helplessness in their men in order to feel needed, to give themselves a role in life. They feared that if left to themselves, men would simply forsake them altogether for life in the company of each other and the bottle.

The whole depressing cycle became clear to me one evening when I was a guest at a birthday dinner. A jovial father told anecdotes as he clinked glasses with his son. The mother wore the look of long-suffering boredom that Russian women adopt when their men are drinking. She must have heard the jokes a hundred times before. All the while, she fussed over her son, stroking his hair and smiling indulgently at her little trainee drinker.

Girls are desperate to escape their alcoholic fathers and weary mothers, but since flats are not allocated to single women without children, they see marriage as the only way to gain some independence. Even so, many married couples live for years with one set of parents or in-laws. At first the bride feels bolstered by the status of "married." If the husband likes the occasional session with his mates she thinks there is nothing wrong with that, for in her experience all men do the same thing. She is tolerant. Their child is born. Life becomes harder. The husband escapes into the bottle more often. The wife is bored and disillusioned with him. She concentrates on her child for emotional fulfillment. She often hits the bottle herself.

If a woman has a daughter she will train her to do housework and look after men. If she has a son she indulges him, does her best to ensure he eats a lot of meat, and turns a blind eye when he begins drinking heavily. When he behaves badly she cries with pride, "He is a man!"

Women believe their domain is the home and that it is their natural role in life to look after drunken husbands and sons. In a society which excludes them from political power it is the one element of control they feel they have.

Since the time of Peter the Great Russian governments have attempted to curb alcoholism. Worried by alcohol-related absenteeism from work, Gorbachev introduced the hugely unpopular dry laws in the 1980s. The poet Yevtushenko warned of their human consequences:

"State vodka and wine, which have dropped significantly in quality over recent years but are still more or less quality-controlled, have yielded to moonshine made out of the-devil-knows-what, including lotions and callus removers. This will have and already has had horrifying genetic repercussions. What will a child be like conceived under the effects of anti-freeze?"[5]

Samogon killed and blinded thousands. Between 1986 and 1989 a million people were convicted of moonshining and there was loss of revenue from state-controlled vodka sales that yielded a budget deficit. This was the beginning of the end for Gorbachev.

Yevtushenko suggested that the worst effects of alcoholism would be eased by the availability of good-quality drink. These days there is an ocean of imported liquor on sale in private shops, but few can afford it. The new class of businessmen now rot their livers with scotch while the majority continue to swig adulterated vodka, *samogon* and eau de Cologne.

In 1994 dozens of people in the neighbouring town of Syzran dropped dead from alcohol poisoning. They had waylaid a goods train and broken into a wagon of industrial alcohol. To my mind, this was desperation on a par with 18th century London when Gordon rioters fell dead as they drank the gin coursing through the Holborn gutters.

---

[5] Y. Yevtushenko: *Fatal Half Measures* (Little, Brown and Company, 1991) p. 134.

Historically, times of social turbulence in Russia have been accompanied by an upsurge of drunkenness. It increased in the 1860s with the liberation of serfs, then decreased during the relatively stable 1880s. It rose again in 1905 and after 1917, despite Bolshevik attempts to curb it. There has been a marked rise in alcoholism since the collapse of communism, with a resulting decrease in male life expectancy.

The attraction of vodka in a cold country is understandable. Boswell described spirits as "a means to supply by art the want of that genial warmth of blood which the sun produces." If Russians have learned to takes nips of vodka to warm frozen limbs they have also learned to swill it to blot out the pain of everyday life.

The Russian way of drinking is to imbibe a lot of strong alcohol as quickly as possible. I thought them poor drinking companions, for I am used to the leisurely drinking culture of southern Europe, where people rarely lose control. In Samara the whole point was to lose control. Drinkers went through wild mood swings which all too often resulted in outbursts of aggression.

Violence is an accepted part of Russian drinking culture. Lina Ivanovna said there was a common belief that a wedding was not a wedding without a good brawl. A few years ago she had been a guest at one where a barrel of *samogon* was brought in from the country. Two men and a woman dropped dead from alcohol poisoning. The other guests called an ambulance which took the corpses away to a mortuary. Then they carried on drinking and fighting. Next morning they faced each other with black eyes and bruises to begin drinking again. Two men started a fight at the top of the stairs; they tumbled down and one was killed. Again an ambulance had to be called. The next day those who had drunk themselves to death were brought back in coffins. Another barrel of *samogon* was fetched from the country and the revelry resumed.

In pre-revolutionary Russia there were many Orthodox holy days which gave serfs the opportunity to indulge themselves with vodka. When the Soviet regime rearranged the calendar, Workers' Day (May 1st) and Revolution Day (November 7th) became occasions for drunkenness, murder and mayhem. Criminologists in the 1920s, concerned over the amount of fighting on holidays in rural areas, traced the custom back to feast days of old when drunken boyars would challenge each other over real or imagined slights to their honour. The early Soviet government vainly tried to combat rural violence with a deluge of atheist propaganda.

International Women's Day is a public holiday in Russia. A female acquaintance called on me, suggesting we celebrate. I did not feel like drinking, so I made the excuse that I was about to go out. My friend insisted on staying in my room until I returned, saying that she had to wait for her boyfriend. Paralysed by my English desire to remain polite at all costs, and loathe to banish her outside to wait in the snow, I agreed. I returned three hours later to find the girl and three men in an advanced state of intoxication. Three empty vodka bottles rolled around the floor of my room. When I showed them the door one of the men, a fellow of neanderthal physique, swore and pushed me away. Boris emerged from his room down the corridor to see what was going on. Apeman ran at him, punched him in the face and knocked him to the ground. The other two joined in, kicking Boris repeatedly in the head. He screamed until he lost consciousness.

When a burly neighbour opened his door our attackers

stumbled off into the night. I called an ambulance, which took forty minutes to arrive. A man and woman in white coats entered the flat and pulled Boris roughly to his feet.

"Name? Age? Address?" barked the woman. I assumed they were testing his memory, but discovered that forms had to be filled in before we could go anywhere.

I accompanied Boris to the casualty ward of a state hospital. The staff were busy that night because of the holiday celebrations. They were marginally less rude after blood and urine samples showed no trace of alcohol in Boris's system. Seats and trolleys were piled with blood-caked figures, male and female. It looked as if a riot had just taken place rather than a public holiday. While I waited for Boris to be assigned a bed a young girl came up and leaned against him. She had a blood-soaked bandage around her head and was quite drunk.

"At least he has a friend to help him," she said at last. "Come back for me!" she shouted after us down the corridor.

The next day I had to make a police report. I was shunted from pillar to post; no member of Samara's finest wanted anything to do with me. My status as a foreigner meant paperwork for them. The FSK (formerly the KGB) sent me to the central police headquarters, who in turn directed me to my local station. Here, in a little cubbyhole at the entrance to a block of flats, a lugubrious police captain sat under a bust of Felix Dzerzhinsky. When he saw my passport he leapt out of his seat and into the corridor. I heard raised voices:

"Comrade Major, there's an Englishwoman involved in this. Never in my life . . . I mean, you are my senior, please . . ."

"Comrade Captain, you have been delegated to handle this case."

"Comrade Major, I beg you . . ."

A dejected captain returned and arranged to come to my

flat to study the scene of the crime.

He called at seven the following morning and spent a long time examining the hole in the wall made by the kicks that Boris's head had failed to intercept. He left looking even more depressed. Later Boris explained that a shot of vodka would have been the decent and expected thing to offer.

The next day Boris and I were called to give statements at the central police station. The captain arrived late and somewhat unsteadily. Did I know the best vodka in the world was made locally? Why on earth had I let those riff-raff into my room for a drinking session? I obviously did not understand the Russian way of drinking.

As we left we passed a group of police hauling in some drunks from the railway station next door. They were thrown into a metal cage in the corner of a room, men and women together. A woman's slurred voice reached me down the urine-scented corridor. She was telling her mates a joke about the unnatural relations between Winnie the Pooh and Piglet.

I felt I had just walked through a scene from a pre-revolution novel, yet each year between ten and fifteen per cent of Russia's adult population pass through similar sobering-up cells.

In order to press charges Boris needed a certificate of injury but the hospital which treated him refused to provide this. Instead, for reasons that never became clear, we were sent to the city mortuary, a lonely building in a frozen field near the river. Directed to room 106, we knocked and entered. Inside sat a tiny man in a white coat, surrounded by four female mannequins. Three were crowned with shimmering gold wigs, the fourth with a mass of auburn curls.

"You're in the wrong place, you want the old mortuary," he shrieked, red-faced with rage.

The old mortuary greeted us with the familiar padded doors and lavatorial odours common to all Russian public institutions. A pathologist told us to go back to the first building, by which time Boris had decided against proving his head injury. "If it goes on record that I suffered concussion I might lose my gun licence. I'll settle for lesser charges."

His gun had been stolen the week before his attack. I mentally blessed the thief. The incident could have been far worse.

A month later the police informed us they had caught our malefactors and we were summoned to a preliminary court hearing. Judge Yashin flipped through the file with shaking hands. He picked his nose and stuck a match between his teeth.

"Under article 212 of the Criminal Code your attackers will be fined 100 roubles if found guilty."

That is less than eight pence. Boris and I decided to put the matter down to experience.

Later Apeman went to Boris to apologise, attributing his behaviour to drunkenness. It transpired that Apeman's girlfriend owed a large sum of money to Boris, and Apeman resented him for this.

The women to whom I related the saga showed concern, but asked what could be expected when men got together to drink? If women were not particularly surprised by the incident, it led me to wonder about the level of domestic violence they commonly experience. It is not a subject that receives much public airing, yet studies in the 1960s showed that the majority of prisoners in jail had been found guilty of hooliganism, and nearly half of these had been sentenced for wife-beating.[6]

---

[6] V. Chalidze: *Criminal Russia* (Random House, 1977) p. 98.

Despite the official silence on the subject there is no reason to believe that domestic violence in Russia is any less prevalent than it is in Britain or the US. As in the West 20 years ago, it is not considered a fit subject for study or discussion. When alcoholism is criticised in the press it is condemned as a cause of absenteeism and the impoverishment of women and children. Women still think of domestic violence as a private problem and too shameful to discuss in public. Others hold the even more debased view that it is natural male behaviour and not worthy of discussion. As men are not believed to be masters of their own actions, they are excused.

One cannot pass unscathed through a land of serious drinkers, but one learns to adapt. In London I avoid the Old Kent Road at pub chucking-out time. In France I do not ride a motorbike in mid-afternoon when drivers are returning from lunch. Similarly, in Russia I keep away from alcoholic gatherings and I check the sobriety of my neighbours before taking a seat on a tram. Once I was grabbed by a drunk sitting next to me—he let go in surprise when I shouted in English. The other passengers stared out of the window as Londoners do when something unpleasant is happening on the tube.

There is a difference between coping with drunks in public and living with one. I asked Lina Ivanovna why so many women put up with their alcoholic husbands. "For money," she replied. "Their salaries are lower than men's and it's usually not enough to support themselves and a child."

On average women earn 30% less than men, and it is extremely hard to survive on the little they earn. Even so, the wife and child may never see the man's wage before it is blown on drink. Yet the reasons for female complicity with male drunkenness go beyond economics. If it is a product of poverty and housing shortages, it also stems from low self-esteem and the tradition of passivity. They will not challenge alcoholism in themselves or in men until they glimpse brighter alternatives, and most have never seen a society where mass drunkenness is not the norm.

Women do constantly complain to each other about their useless spouses who blow their wages on drink. I sat in on several bitching sessions around bottles of banana liqueur, but these conclaves depressed me for they seemed only to reinforce the status quo. Women listen to their friends' sufferings in order to reassure themselves that the problem is universal rather than individual. If the situation is hopeless then nothing need be done about it.

Cramped flats, poverty, boredom and vodka are a lethal cocktail. Eighty percent of divorces are initiated by women, with alcoholism most often cited as the cause of marital breakdown. Yet the majority of women stay with their alcoholic husbands. Perhaps cynicism underlies the lethargy; if all men drink there is no point in exchanging one drunk in your flat for another.

Women have two basic ways of coping when their husbands come home drunk: they tuck them up or lock them out. Husbands themselves sometimes leave home if they think they have found another woman who will cosset rather than banish them until they sober up.

Like their Western counterparts, Russian women are also inculcated with the idyll of romance. In the West however, a woman is encouraged to do everything in her power to rectify a conjugal life that falls short of expectations, whereas Russian culture promotes stoicism in women. At most, an unhappy wife in Samara will run over to Lina Ivanovna's for a card-reading session. For many, it is too much trouble to throw out their drunken man and start again, regardless of the fact that life with the drunkard causes enormous stress. Lina Ivanovna was one of the few women I knew who considered living alone to be her best option. Yet even she spent many hours advising young women on catching and keeping men.

A well-known character in 19th Russian literature was the "superfluous man." Exemplified by Goncharov's *Oblomov*, he was typically a noble who rejected both state service and the sybaritic Court life. While serfs laboured and bureaucrats ordered, the superfluous man dedicated himself to day-dreaming and idle speculation.

Lenin set out to destroy the Oblomovs, but the Soviet system created a new order of superfluous people to take their place. While it was illegal not to work and a person unemployed for more than four months could be gaoled for parasitism, most workers simply went through the motions of labour. "We pretend to work and they pretend to pay" was a well-worn saying. When conditions eased after Stalin's death, people simply poured their energies into cultivating private plots or running black market businesses.

Men cope with the tedium of their existences by organizing their lives around the bottle. They crawl into traps of their own design, behaving like petty Oblomovs in the home. Sprawling in front of the television, they let their wives run around cooking and clearing up, as though the latter were genetically programmed to do the housework. Each sex acts out a parody of masculinity or femininity in an attempt to give definition to futile lives.

Nowadays some young women are beginning to voice discontent with men who just look for housekeepers and who behave like "second children." As in the West, there is a trend towards single motherhood and a disinclination to look for a partner for life. Women are becoming more inclined to discard a husband who does not come up to scratch.

Dostoevsky said that man is adaptable, that he grows accustomed to everything. Long ago Russian men and women adapted themselves to life with the help of a vodka bottle. Today they have grown accustomed to a drinking culture. Indeed, it hardly occurs to those who have been isolated for so long, as the Samarans have, to imagine their dipsomaniac society as anything other than normal.

Easter Sunday is a public holiday, the day on which everyone goes to cemeteries armed with vodka bottles to toast their dead. On this day I saw the entire city surrender itself to alcoholic carousal. Lina Ivanovna's son, returning from church, said even the priests were drunk. The Georgians who lived across the road were smashing bottles in the street. At dusk I went for a walk. Kiosks were being mobbed by drunks desperate to refuel. One shack had its windows smashed. Behind it a man was banging another man's head against a wall. No one took any notice. The main street was a magnificent procession of drunks returning from the graveyard. The air reeked of spirits. A few figures stumbled along unaided, clutching bottles. Most passed by in threes: a man in the middle, supported on either side by his wife and mother, each trio a perfect symbol of Russian family life.

The Idiocy of Everyday Life

"Do you think women in the West have any concept of the joys of life? Can they understand the delight of the girl who has managed to buy a bra in her own size by skipping the queue or the joy of the housewife who has 'shot' a kilo of smoked sausage for the holiday?"
JULIA VOZNESENSKAYA: *The Women's Decameron.*

Nothing had prepared me for the senseless tedium and hardship of Russian daily life. Of course I did not live as a Russian woman does. I was free from the need to care for a husband and children. For a few hours a week teaching English I received the equivalent of a factory worker's wages. Most important, I carried a different culture in my head, with the knowledge that I could return to it when I had had enough. On the other hand I lacked the infrastructure of family and friends that is so vital to survival. It was frustrating to constantly appeal for guidance through the Byzantine intricacies of bureaucracy. Most of the time I felt like Alice, battling through a looking-glass world whose rules I did not understand.

Shopping took up a large part of each day. At first I tried to render queuing bearable by bringing a book or newspaper with me. Unfortunately it is impossible to have a quiet read in a Russian queue. One is pushed and jostled and dug in the ribs by importunate old ladies who want to know what is on display and how much it costs. Russians do not share the British respect for privacy and personal space. Although this means they are free from the more bizarre neuroses of our repressive society, I found it makes for an uncomfortable public life. It unsettled me to stand in a queue while a tiny *babushka* tried to burrow past my bottom to peer through the glass of the display counter.

People constantly shouted questions to assistants over the heads of waiting customers, yet prices were clearly marked on the front of the counter. At first I wondered whether everyone was terribly short-sighted, or perhaps illiterate; finally I understood that in Russia shopping is a social activity and any opportunity for conversation or argument is gratefully seized upon. I was often asked to explain the contents of tins and jars. One lady, spying a red plastic bottle of Hungarian tomato ketchup, roared in my ear, "What's that, shampoo?"

Usually I avoided queues by shopping in the market where a greater selection of produce was available for higher prices. I was lucky to be rich enough to do this. But sometimes there was no help for it but to queue in state shops. I set out one day to buy cheese. There was none in the first five dairies I tried. Eventually I spotted a greasy yellow block in a grocery shop. The queue was reasonably short but as I reached its head the shop assistant turned her back. A young porter was dragging cartons in from a back room which the girl started to unpack. As she arranged the contents on the shelves behind her she joked with the porter and ignored the waiting customers.

Although tempted to walk out of the shop and eat plain potatoes again for dinner, I steeled myself to push for victory. I turned to join another queue where an assistant was doling out butter into polythene bags proffered by customers. She would probably refuse to serve me with cheese if it were not her domain, but I hoped to persuade her with a display of foreigner's confusion. I waited another ten minutes while the queue lengthened. Suddenly the second girl turned to help her colleague stack sausage. A drunk at the back shouted at the girls to stop stacking and start serving.

"I've been on my feet eight hours," he yelled.

One of the girls turned around and said, with a look of utter indifference, "So have I."

Then a fight started as a hefty middle-aged woman tried to push in and the drunk objected. Several people began to pummel each other. The drunk eventually triumphed by seizing upon a frail old *babushka* and persuading the assistant to serve her out of turn. He also slipped in his order, whereupon I began to seethe with resentment. I tried to catch the attention of other shoppers, rolling my eyes and flashing a long-suffering smile at the army officer behind me. No one acknowledged my grimaces. Feeling foolish, I pulled myself together and stared impassively ahead with the rest. After 40 minutes in the shop I finally bought my cheese. I left with a throbbing head and hatred for the entire nation. I felt sorely tempted to follow the Russian example and hit the bottle as soon as I reached home.

As I turned the key to my room a neighbour came shuffling down the corridor to see what I had bought. Like many women, she found other people's shopping an endless topic of speculation and intrigue.

"I queued 40 minutes for this," I said, brandishing my packet.

"That's nothing. Try it for four hours."

I vowed never to put myself through that again, preferring to go without the food I wanted. For five months I drank no milk because I refused to rise at half past six in the morning and stand in the freezing street waiting for my container to be filled. I bought produce at random. If there was no queue for a product, I bought it. It became possible to avoid the worst queues by adopting a flexible diet; I once asked a friend why more people did not do the same.

"Because we cannot live without our daily bread and sausage. If we were vegetarian like you we would fade away and die. Our lives involve so much heavy physical labour we need meat to fortify ourselves. Especially men."

If the meaning of triumph is finding three rolls of toilet paper after six weeks of scouring the shops, the essence of despair is seeing sour cream on sale for the first time in a month and realising you have left the necessary glass jar at home. For many products you have to supply your own container.

At times I was blinded by homicidal rage when the person in front of me dithered about, wanting 50 grammes taken off her lump of butter, or asking for her leaking kefir bottle to be replaced. The person at the head of the queue takes full advantage of her position while those behind her suffer.

I wondered why Russians so doggedly subject themselves to the soul-destroying experience of queuing. No one can remember a time when it was not the norm, and no one can break the habit of a lifetime. As in the days of rationing in Britain, a queue is joined because it is there. People hope to find a scarce or cheap item at the other end. I was the rebel without an ounce of *priterpelost* whose criterion for buying a product was the shortness of the queue for it.

Some shops still work on the archaic system of ordering, paying and collecting at different points, which meant queuing three times. You queue to pay at a cashier's desk before taking your receipt back to the counter to collect your purchases. This dates from Tsarist days when assistants were not expected to be literate or able to handle change, but the Soviet regime never thought to rationalise the process of shopping. That way more people could be provided with employment.

The only thing that kept my blood pressure down during shopping forays was the charm of certain shop assistants. They would ask where I was from, guessing from my strange clothes and accent that I was Latvian or Estonian. On learning that I was English they would exclaim with pleasure. I always returned to those shops where otherwise dour faces broke into smiles:

"Here comes our Englishwoman!"

Only once a woman in the queue behind me muttered, "That's right, give the best stuff to the foreigner."

Another "foreigner," a descendant of Polish settlers, said that I was merely receiving all-the-better-to-cheat-you-with smiles, but I was past caring. Let them give me short measures, I thought, if only a drop of human kindness falls on me while out shopping today.

It is not easy to find shops. In the suburbs they are located on the ground floor of apartment blocks, and from the outside they look like just another flat with no indication of their function. I only came upon them by following other shoppers. These sort of places only sell a limited selection of products. I might have to visit four different shops to buy bread, cheese, eggs and tea. In winter it took an age to hobble across the frozen wastelands between blocks. A thousand feet had pressed the snow into packed ice. At times I had to ask passers-by to assist me down slopes which threatened my purchases and my bones.

While making my feeble way along the slippery streets I laughed bitterly at *Rock for Privatisation* posters. The collapse of the Soviet system means roads do not get cleared as they used to. Like almost everything else, salting, gritting and ice-breaking services are in abeyance, awaiting privatisation. Walking is dangerous, especially for the old. There was a dairy across the road at the end of Specialist Alley and an old neighbour woman used to stand like a sentry in the entranceway to Number Four. If she saw me returning from the dairy she would ask what they had on sale that day. She was not going to risk her limbs by crossing the road to find that, as usual, the shop had no sugar, butter or sour cream. Either there had been no deliveries or the assistants had put the best stuff aside for their cronies. The situation became so absurd that one morning I had to tell the old lady the grim truth that there was nothing but caviare in the shop.

Privatisation has not made shopping easier for the majority of the population. In the city centre Samarans could buy 57 varieties of imported liquor, including, God help them, cans of English sparkling strawberry wine. They could purchase a video recorder, French perfume or canisters of CS gas. Yet they still have to queue for milk, fruit, vegetables and soap, if they can afford them in the first place.

All shops close for a lunch hour; the problem is that they choose different times to do this. As it was hard to remember which shops closed when, many of my shopping forays ended in frustration. If the shop was not closed for lunch it might be shut for cleaning, repair or for no reason at all. Sometimes I arrived at shops to find them bolted and barred, with the sound of delivery men carousing with the assistants inside.

Delivery is chaotic. These days no one wants to work for minimum wages as a van driver or porter. Conscript soldiers are sometimes called in to distribute bread throughout the city. This results in shortages and long queues when bread finally arrives.

One day I found a supermarket. It was built in the finest Soviet nuclear-bunker style of architecture with no external indication of its function. Inside, the vast hangar boasted little trolleys, checkouts and all of a dozen different products on sale. One aisle was devoted to three-litre jars of gherkins, another to Azerbaijani tomato paste, a third to mock caviare made from pumpkin. Every product came in giant sizes; my weakness limited me to one jar per visit. Local women stoically lugged their bags home, for none had cars.

Two girls stood by the doors peering into shoppers' bags as they left. They checked off goods bought against receipts. This farce was a hangover from Soviet days. While the assistants subjected shoppers to this scrutiny, truckloads of goods were going out via the back door to be sold on the black market.

Many women had to use their lunch break for shopping in this supermarket, so after midday fresh produce is sold out and customers arriving after work face empty shelves. On evenings and weekends there were long queues for cheese, kefir, fish and meat. I was in the shop one day when a consignment of frozen chicken arrived. Women hurtled towards the freezer with their trolleys, pushing and shoving each other to grab a scrawny fowl. I walked out in disgust. Later I rationalised that it is the system that reduces human beings to this level, but my immediate feeling was one of nausea. The women in the supermarket were not starving, they simply had the misfortune to live under a system which deprived its citizens unnecessarily, pitting one human against another. A friend put it bluntly: "If we lived under British conditions we could behave like civilized human beings too."

During these months I noticed changes in my own psyche which helped me empathise with those around me. Intellectual activity was pushed aside to make way for more basic concerns such as what I was going to have for dinner. Each day I would start out with my empty bottles and polythene bags, hoping to find something edible to buy. It was a victory if by the end of the day I could procure yoghurt, mineral water or eggs. Compared to these small triumphs a woman who fights for and grabs a frozen chicken must return home like a conquering hero.

While out shopping I thought wistfully of Boris's abortive attempt to open a Pizza outlet. It would have provided a welcome service in this city where there is nowhere for tired shoppers to stop for a cup of tea and a rest. Women stay on their feet until they have filled their bags, which they then heave onto public transport for the journey home.

Occasionally I went to a public dining room for shop and office workers. These unfortunates had to spend half their lunch hour on their feet queuing for bowls of fatty soup and stew. Clutching a sticky tray, I would join the line, pick up a battered aluminum dish of sauerkraut and a hunk of bread, and wait an age for the cashier to tot up each bill on her abacus.

At first, when I was still in my foreign-voyeur stage, I was entranced by the dining room's clientèle. Once again I felt as though I had stepped back into a past epoch. Old Tolstoy peasants with matted locks and beards sat at tables in felt boots and shaggy goat-skin coats. They came from remote farms across the Volga, in winter trudging across the frozen river pulling sledges loaded with produce for sale in the city. Gypsy women in multi-coloured skirts and headscarves sashayed amongst the tables cadging money off diners. By summer the thrill of exotica had died; I felt worn down by the heat and stench and longed only to eat my food in peace.

Having shopped and bought enough food to prepare some sort of evening meal, I would have to wait for up to an hour for a bus or tram home. Transport was intolerably crowded during rush hour. I took care to avoid the inevitable gaggle of drunks huddled at the back of the vehicle. At any time of day, even six in the morning, the tram would contain at least one vodka-sodden man having an argument with himself.

Almost as bad as the drunks were the guardians of social order in the front section of the tram. In their opinion I had no right to a seat unless I was pregnant (they would not hesitate to ask). Once I was strap-hanging, gazing out of the window, when I felt a tap on my shoulder: "Face forward! Better for us, better for you!" a vigilant citizeness chanted in my ear. Everyone knew that foreigners were spies.

I would reach home with frazzled nerves, sometimes only to find that the water or electricity had been turned off without warning. Kind neighbours lent me buckets to fill at the street pump. They said they were used to this occurrence. The entire city spent the summer of 1991 without hot water "for technical reasons."

My neighbours laughed at my raptures over the old fairytale wooden houses in our district. Boris explained: "They have no baths, toilets, or running water. Each hut houses two families. The two-storey houses have a family in each room. Only the very poor, the old, refugees and assorted riff-raff live in those. Ninety per cent of the inhabitants of the houses in our street have no official jobs. Most of them are 'blacks.' They work the markets, peddling drugs under the fruit counters. They drink, racketeer..."

Prejudice against "blacks"—people from the Caucasus—was rife. One day I was shopping in the central covered market when police burst in with guns drawn to round up "foreigners" (I am blonde—they did not ask to see my passport). On the pretext of clamping down on crime Yeltsin had ordered Caucasians and Central Asians to be rounded up and sent back to their "own" countries. Shoppers looked on impassively. No one protested as Georgian and Azerbaijani stall-holders were hauled off.

As winter drew in I saw the reality of life in our district. At the end of each street water taps protruded through hummocks of ice. I could not get near the taps without slipping over on these miniature glaciers. Yet old women relentlessly trudged back and forth with metal pails. So much for picturesque surroundings. This vestige of old Russia destroyed the last of my romantic illusions about the past.

Russian sewers cannot cope with lavatory paper. Every toilet has a bucket beside it for waste. In apartment buildings these buckets have to be emptied down a chute on the communal landing. But air blows up this chute, so as one tips the bucket the dirty paper is caught in the up-draught and flies all over the place. One is then faced with the revolting task of retrieving these bits of paper and depositing them one by one down the chute. Food waste goes the same way. All rubbish falls into a cubicle on the ground floor of the block. Stray dogs and cats scavenge these dumps. These kept the rats down; I only saw one rat outside Number Four. Once a week a man would turn up with a shovel and cart, unlock the cubicle door, and dig away at the stinking mound inside. Waste disposal from the old wooden houses was even more primitive. Every evening an open cart drove slowly through the streets. Residents would run out with their waste buckets and hand them up to be emptied by a man standing amidst the filth in the cart.

Residents of my tenement washed their bodies at the public bath house and their clothes in tubs of water boiled up on stoves. They envied those who lived in *micro-raioni* flats with bathrooms and running hot water on tap. Yet in these flats women still did all their washing in the bath tub. There were one or two laundries in the city, but I was warned that they rarely returned a garment in one piece.

By any standards Russian women are well-groomed; given the conditions under which they live they work miracles. An elegant friend explained that in spring she cleaned her coat and boots every morning before going out. She said she had to, for the melting snow turns streets into rivers of mud. Drains are unable to cope with the meltwater. Drivers speed past bus stops, taking their revenge on humanity by spraying the queues.

I saw no point in cleaning my boots every day to have them dirtied again as soon as I stepped outside. In the end I was shamed into conformity. Footwear is taken off at the entrance to flats and left by the front door; if I did not clean my own boots I would often find someone else had done it for me. It was hard to be a rebel in Samara.

Urban women pay a great deal of attention to their appearance. They are always admiring each others' clothes and enquiring where to find a particular material or pattern. They had high hopes of me, wanting to know which perfumes were fashionable in the West, and how to wax their legs. They were disappointed by my ignorance of these matters, and discreetly shocked by my appearance. Even the man's watch I wore was a matter for comment.

Some Samarans had heard about the weird habits of foreigners. A librarian breathlessly asked me if it was true that

German women wore no make-up. She could not have been more shocked if she heard they walked around naked. Most young Samaran girls looked like entrants in a "Miss Iowa 1962" contest, in their careful masks of thick foundation, blusher and lipstick. Hair was arranged in peroxide puffs. High heels were mandatory in all but the worst weather.

As the months passed I felt a deepening sense of isolation from the world. My reality was composed of ice-bound streets and tiny over-heated rooms; my horizons confined to the Volga and the purple distance of vast steppeland. It was an effort to keep in touch with the outside world. A phone call to London or Moscow meant a trek down to the international exchange and a queue for a booth. Post from abroad took two to three weeks, if it arrived at all. National newspapers could take a week to reach Samara from Moscow. Local papers consisted of advertisements and horoscopes. "International affairs" on TV usually concerned meetings between world leaders.

If this was post-communist freedom of information I hated to think of the darkness in which Samarans had been kept before *perestroika*. Yet considering their isolation, many were remarkably well informed about the outside world. I have encountered more ignorance and parochialism in California, where there was no excuse.

As a result of a literary diet of Dickens and Sherlock Holmes Samarans pictured Britain as a foggy island crowded with 19th century characters. I had to laugh at myself, for my own image of Russia had been formed by a diet of pre-revolution literature. Each day in Samara forced me to re-examine my illusions about Russia.

Most of the people I met were conscious of themselves as Samarans almost before they were Russians. They had a vision of themselves living in a state whose boundaries ended somewhere beyond Toliatti in the north and Chapaevsk to the south. Most had been to Moscow for shopping and the Black Sea for a holiday, but in the past only "reliable" citizens had been allowed to go abroad, usually to Eastern Europe. Now this is changing and anyone with the means can travel overseas. However, visits to Western Europe necessitate long queues and interviews at embassies in Moscow. Most foreign tours have to be bought with dollars, which makes them the privilege of the new *biznesmeni*. The purpose of their trips is usually to stock up on electronics from Turkey or the U.A.E. Travel is regarded as little more than a shopping opportunity. Valentina, the woman in London who had invited me to Samara, said that when she returned for a short visit to her family she had been besieged by old friends: "Almost everyone I had ever known called on me. They were so anxious to see what I had brought back. Only one person actually asked what Britain was *like*." After a few months in Samara I began to understand this hunger for material acquisition. I returned from a week's break in Moscow quite excited over my purchases of green peppers, eyeshadow, sunglasses and a tin of seaweed.

The conversation of most of the women in Specialist Alley revolved around what was in the shops and how much it cost. I began to fear that my own interests were shrinking to this level. I felt my intellect drying up as my physical needs became all-consuming. From November to April I was preoccupied with the need to quell hunger pangs or to find shelter from the freezing cold of the streets. I thought wistfully of my cerebral life in the West, where access to food was never a problem for me. How easy it used to be to take care of my body's needs so that I could concentrate on the life of my mind—and how little I appreciated this at the time. In Samara I was unable to dwell in my head for too long; hunger or physical pain from the cold always pulled me back to reality. Increasingly, I came to understand the use of vodka as a barrier against cold, hunger and misery.

Yet summer provided a respite from the daily treadmill. As the July temperatures rose to 90 degrees the city's population poured down to sandy riverbanks. Even women snatched a few days away from work on their dachas to relax by the Volga. Families stayed in beach huts and holiday camps subsidised by factories. These peaceful camps had none of the organised jollity of their Western counterparts. A friend took me to stay in one that belonged to the aluminium factory where her parents worked. We slept in wooden cabins dotted amongst pine trees. At night I heard the whispers of children creeping up to my hut: "This is where the Englishwomen lives!"

We sunbathed on beaches, watching oil tankers, barges and pleasure boats ply upriver to Moscow or down to Astrakhan on the Caspian Sea. "Mafia cruises," said my friend of the pleasure boats.

We spent radiant days swimming in the warm Volga. My friend's elderly parents took me out walking in the fields. As we gathered cornflowers her father serenaded his wife with Chaliapin arias. Later that evening we sat over a bottle of *samogon* and he sang the praises of Stalin

Back in my warm London flat it is easy to recall fond images of Samara: the day I triumphantly steered a ferry down the Volga, the smell of wet birch leaves in the bath house, and the overwhelming kindness of friends. Perhaps it is like the aftermath of childbirth, when the brain suppresses memories of pain, for it is harder to recall those times when my feet turned numb at the bus-stop, when the bones in my fingers ached intolerably, and drunks pushed me aside as the tram arrived. Yet it was experiences such as these that gave me an understanding of just how heavy a physical, mental and spiritual toll Russian daily life exacts upon its citizens.

"We Women are Used to Pain"

"The upper strata of society, especially numerous in the centres, have produced the type of elegant and indolent lady, who follows the fashions, the theatre, the concerts, who is desolated when she is unable to get the latest dance records from abroad, who tans herself every year on the beaches of the Crimea . . . Below this feminine aristocracy is the average housewife of modest means, as needy as she is everywhere else. Still lower—and she constitutes the majority—is the woman of the people, a worker or peasant, who does the washing, goes for water to the fountain or the river (in winter, it is to a hole punctured in the ice), takes care of the animals, raises the children, receives the drunken man at the end of the week, stands in line in front of the stores, buys a few metres of satinette in order to resell them, and, thanks to this brilliant stroke of business, is able to provide shoes for the youngest. The foreign litterateurs do not come to question her while travelling. Disfigured and aged at thirty-five, she sometimes takes to drink."

VICTOR SERGE: *Destiny of a Revolution*

Life for provincial Russian women has changed little since this description was written in the thirties. Class distinctions have altered more in detail than substance. The mafia wife might now acquire her tan in Sri Lanka rather than the Crimea. Since the collapse of the planned economy the means of the average housewife have become so modest that she now spends her weekends standing out in the biting cold peddling clothes and toilet paper. The woman on the *kolkhoz* or in a private sector house perpetually trudges to the tap in the street. Alcohol is still the favoured escape route.

The Soviet economy was largely built by female labour. The country had to industrialise in order to establish the material preconditions for socialism. Industry needed workers and the workers had to be fed. Consequently women were drawn into factories, fields and canteens. In 1928 28% of the paid workforce was female; by 1987 this had risen to 51%. Soviet women had the highest rate of employment in the world. Liberation from the petty drudgery of domestic work gave them the freedom to go out to work all day before coming home to do all the housework.

The country's sweated labour is predominantly female. Male workers shuffle pieces of paper while women wield the hoe and the shovel. The hardest, dirtiest jobs in agriculture and industry fall to women, yet on average they earn 70% of the male wage. Since 1991 they have borne the brunt of unemployment; their jobs are regarded as more expendable than men's.

Daily life for all but the elite is an endless round of drudgery. Housework has always been considered an exclusively female domain. This double burden of paid work and domestic labour takes its toll: female life expectancy is seven to ten years lower than in Western Europe.

At an official level there has never been any questioning of sex roles or any attempt to divide tasks equally. When those on high discussed the double burden it was part of an attempt to get women back to the home. This drive began a few decades ago when the government became concerned about falling birth rates in European Russia. In 1970 new labour legislation extended maternity leave and stipulated that pregnant women be moved to lighter work. In theory, labour such as that performed by Lina Ivanovna's sister would not now be permitted. However, by 1990 at least four million women were still working in conditions that contravened this legislation. Health and safety inspectors are not immune from bribery. If a woman complains or suffers as a result of her working conditions she faces dismissal, or even—in the case of Boris's mother—incarceration in a lunatic asylum.

When economic incentives to reproduce proved too mean to have any effect the government launched a propaganda drive. It was alleged that the basis of a woman's personality is her natural urge to give birth. There were even hints that childlessness could lead to insanity. Central Asian women did not fit this model, apparently. Worried about the high birthrate there, the Soviet government lauded women's economic and political achievements rather than the joys of motherhood.

This propaganda campaign failed to produce the three children per woman that the government deemed appropriate for European Russia. During the 1980s the tendency to have smaller families increased, as did the divorce rate and the number of single-parent families. The government responded by launching a family values campaign. Gorbachev urged women to see themselves first and foremost as wives and mothers. He spoke of the "purely womanly mission" of homemaking and child-rearing. The breakdown of the family was blamed for male alcoholism and juvenile delinquency. It was argued that if a man took his rightful place at the head of the family he would not have to resort to the bottle. Women were supposed to return to the home and create a happy family atmosphere. Now, at the end of the century, the number of deaths in Russia exceeds the number of births. Women are simply deciding not to have children, blaming the current economic climate for their decisions.

My Samaran friends agreed that the double burden was a terrible strain on their physical and mental health. They said the problem arose from the lack of eligible men, their love of drink and refusal to raise a finger in the house. They believed this attitude was rooted in an "Oriental mentality" which deems domestic labour shameful for a man.

Both men and women thought feminism was something to do with George Sand. Since the 1970s male supremacy has been challenged by a few women's groups in Moscow and St. Petersburg, but Samara has remained closed to such subversion. Basically, women did not expect men to change; they simply devised ways of coping with the help of female friends and relations.

Some women go to the extreme of elevating their servitude to martyrdom. Lina Ivanovna had a friend named Olga Vassilievna, whose husband was an alcoholic. He no longer worked, her daughter was a junkie and her son-in-law was a petty hoodlum who lorded over the household. He even kicked Olga's beloved pet dogs when they got under his feet. She worked night shifts in a weapons factory that masqueraded as a tractor plant. Like many workers she had had to wait months for her wages, due to alleged problems with the Central Bank. At weekends Olga stood for hours in the market, selling jeans that her son-in-law brought down from Kazan. He pocketed any money she earned. Olga took solace in Mexican soap operas, astrology, the Church and card sessions with Lina

Ivanovna. Privately, Lina and I agreed she would do better to evict her useless family, but she had convinced herself they were the cross she had to bear and that there was nothing she could do about the situation.

Olga Vassilievna revelled in the vision of herself as the innocent victim of the malice of others. The Orthodox Church reinforced her attempt to find nobility in suffering. Marxism also exalted the oppressed, but as they patently did not inherit the earth during 70 years of Soviet power, it is not surprising that women are flocking back to the Church.

Like Olga, many Russian women try to retain their self-esteem by extolling their victimhood, gathering in kitchens to pour their hearts out to each other. These kitchen discussions are socially acceptable ways of letting off steam, but through them, women reinforce each other's misery. Once, when I told a group of women that I was suffering from cystitis, one of them sighed and said, "It must be terrible. Still, we women are used to pain, aren't we?"

Young women showed a placid acceptance of their fate. I talked to dozens of female students at Samara's various colleges. They combined intelligence, charm and great curiosity about the outside world with unquestioning conformity to their society's values. They expected to graduate, find a job and be married by the age of 23. Most agreed that 21 was the ideal age for marriage. When asked why they had to marry and marry so young they said it was simply tradition. They expressed a horror of remaining 'blue stockings': their pejorative term for a spinster.

These girls were the products of decades of social isolation. If they never questioned their existences it was because they never suspected that there could be any other way to live. Now cracks are appearing in their enclosed world and intimations of other cultures starting to filter in. Students told me about a German musical troupe who had visited their college: "They were amazing, some were 25 and 26 and they were not at all worried that they were single," said an aspiring photo-model. "If I waited that long I fear no one would want me!"

I guessed that if any student had different plans she might be hesitant to speak up in front of her peers and teachers, so when one of the girls asked to meet me alone I hoped to meet a dissenting spirit.

Zoya was a student living the usual existence in a two-room flat with a drunkard father and a prematurely-aged mother. They were pressurising her to marry, as she was already 21, but she did not fancy adding another drunk to the household. She reminded me of Valentina, my Russian émigré acquaintance in London, with the intensity of her desire to break away from the confines of Samara. Zoya, however, sought a spiritual rather than a material escape route. She had met a group of American Mormons who were trawling her university for converts. They offered answers, a new circle of friends and the prospect of a teetotal American husband. Most of the 20 or so Mormons in town were single men. Zoya said she knew a school teacher who had already married a Mormon and left for Salt Lake City.

The Mormons had taken Zoya to watch a baptism. She had been so impressed by the sight of a large family of Kazakhs being dunked in the Volga that she was now thinking of having herself baptised.

"The Orthodox Church is alienating. The ceremonies are remote. You don't participate. But the Mormons smile in welcome as though they are genuinely happy that I am there. Their music is almost like a disco: they sing together and the atmosphere is of one big family."

I met several other highly-educated women who were attracted to the Mormon faith. The stultification of their lives made them vulnerable to conversion. Samaran society is not kind to girls like Zoya who would rather talk than drink. There is almost nowhere for young people to go when they want to escape their families. When youth do congregate, it is usually with the aim of drinking themselves into a stupor or getting off their heads on solvents. Zoya was impressed by the sobriety and seriousness of the Mormons. They also had the exotic appeal of foreignness. I hoped she would not swap one enclosed life for another.

Zoya's search for a wider world echoed her female ancestors. The great-grandmothers of today's trapped young women also looked to men to help them escape from lives of spiritual desolation. In those days unmarried women were not granted passports. Some entered into fictitious marriages to enable them to leave home, and often, the country. In the latter half of the 19th century nihilist revolutionary groups provided an escape route for educated women. Perhaps history has lent glamour to these sects, but I imagine they offered something more stimulating than American evangelism.

Zoya's friend Anya was scathing about the Mormons. She believed in the Orthodox faith.

"It is part of our ancestral heritage, reaching back a thousand years. How can the Americans come in and give us bibles and expect us to change just like that? I met two American girls last summer. Their trip was financed by the Baptist Church. They gave out bibles at basketball and hockey matches. They were not in the least bit interested in our way of life. They are making a big mistake if they think they can come here and superimpose their beliefs and culture on this society."

Anya worked as an English teacher at a prestigious college. When I first met her she had taken on an additional part-time job, while at night she studied at a new business school. When I ran into her again three months later she looked thin and fraught after a breakdown from overwork and nervous exhaustion. She had been put in the gynaecological ward of a local hospital, which depressed her still further.

"I felt completely isolated there. The other women used to ask how I was feeling but they could not imagine what was going on in my mind. All they could talk about were their husbands and children. I felt very distant from them and sometimes wished I had a baby, too, so I could join in their conversations. I think that is why so many very young girls have babies. They want a reason for living.

"Yes, I know that in reality those women were worn out from looking after their children and alcoholic husbands in overcrowded flats. I want more to my life. I think I am not incompetent, not unattractive, but what is there for me to do? Why do I live like this? I am 25 and still live with my parents. I need a place of my own. I was working seven days a week and I still could not earn enough to gain my independence.

"Do you know why I took that business course? I hoped to meet a man whom I could help with my knowledge of English and business practices. I dreamed of a partnership, a venture we could work in together. As a woman I could not start a business by myself. It is true that many trade as *fartsovki*, but I am too frail to transport heavy baggage by train and sleep third class all the time. Serious business would be more difficult. Do you know who the new businessmen are? Former *Komsomol* and Party members. It is an old boy network. My parents are poor and I have no connections.

"Am I just another Hamlet? I don't know what to do with

myself. I might find fulfilment through creativity. Like the Japanese I could paint and write poetry through pure inspiration, not the desire for money or fame. I considered going abroad, but how would I live there? If no one wants me here who would want me there? It is easier for men, I think. They do not torment themselves with these questions. For them, work is the most important thing in their lives.

"There is nowhere for us to go at night. Socially I mix with my colleagues at work. They are nearly all women. That is another reason I took my extra job—I wanted to meet some men for a change.

"I know that most Russian men are a waste of time. They expect women to be bound by the four walls of their home, busying themselves with housework. Mothers keep their sons in a state of infantilism until middle age. Then their wives take over.

"Men also demand that women look after their emotional needs. For example, a friend of one of my colleagues hanged himself recently. This colleague got drunk and phoned me, wanting reassurance that I cared for him. He phoned again the following evening, and the next. On the fourth night I told him that enough was enough and hung up."

Anya protested more than most. Most young Samaran women conform because they see men as a means of raising their standard of living. Their energies are channelled into catching and keeping a husband. Boris had an admirer who baked cakes for him at any possible opportunity: his birthday, New Year's, Veterans' day. He said it was quite usual for Samaran girls to do this for the men they fancied.

"Girls like her have just one hope in life and that is to get married. She only has a basic education and no official job. She knows how to sew and bake cakes and she hopes that these skills will catch her a husband so she can leave home. Unfortunately she has decided upon me."

Working-class girls seek out their knights even earlier than their educated counterparts. Lina Ivanovna's youngest son Alexei had an 18 year old wife who had been brought up in poverty in a ruinous wooden house. The couple now lived in a room at Number Four. They found it convenient to be near Lina who regularly cooked for them and passed on delicacies presented by grateful clients.

Lina and her daughter-in-law Elena scarcely tolerated each other. It seemed to me that their conflict represented the contrasting aspirations of different generations of women. Lina thought Elena's expectations of life were unrealistically high and grumbled that she blew all her wages on cosmetics while expecting Lina to provide them with food. Elena was remarkably like a western teenager, spending hours dreaming in front of her mirror. Glasnost enabled her to sigh over Kevin Costner and Richard Gere. She had left school at 16 and worked in a clinic taking impressions for false teeth. She was also expected to do all the housework. Alexei, a policeman, insisted on having his tea on the table and the floor washed every day.

Their bitterest rows concerned his German shepherd dog. It was too large an animal to live in one room with them and was constantly making a mess. Elena deeply resented having to clear up after it. Her life as a skivvy contrasted painfully with her self-image. Every few weeks it got too much for her and she ran home to her mother. Alexei would install the dog in Lina's hut for a few days and then go to plead for Elena's return. This gave her a short-lived sense of power, and not having anywhere else to go, she always came back.

Elena belonged to a generation of Russian women whose expectations were higher than those of their mothers or grandmothers. Her discontent was fuelled by television and the sight of luxury Western goods in the shops that she could never afford. She dreamed of riding in a car, something she had only done a few times in her life. She had once been to the Black Sea with a group of Young Pioneers and ever since had longed to return. Her only outing during the past year had been a trip to a collective farm to help with the potato harvest.

Lina's generation suffered the impact of the war. In the fifties men were at a premium; women deemed themselves lucky to catch one at all. Lina's first husband was a petty tyrant who had deserted her sister, yet she still believed, "He was handsome and had a good job. I had no reason to refuse him."

Marriage used to be a practical and economic arrangement, but nowadays girls also expect emotional fulfilment from the union. As they rarely get it, they smother their male children. These grow into men who find it hard to detach themselves from their mothers, and who have unrealistic expectations of their wives.

Younger women take no notice of their worn-out mothers and rush out to sign themselves up as someone's servant for life. They are blind to each other's mistakes. It is as though one had sawn a leg off and then turned to her sisters to assure them that they really are much better off with one leg and that two-leggedness is a truly pitiable state of affairs. When it proves much harder to cope with life they sigh and say this is the price one has to pay for the blissful state of being crippled. Never having known independence, they cling to their belief in men as knights on white chargers who will enable them to escape their families, poverty and powerlessness.

The opening of Samara has prompted a few girls to look for foreign men to rescue them from lives of poverty. Moscow and St. Petersburg have dating agencies which fly in plane-loads of Western men; Samara has not yet reached this level of enterprise. Apart from the Mormons, the other foreign males in the city were Syrian and Moroccan medical students. Some came from wealthy families and were considered good catches by Russian girls. Boris had a friend who married a dental student. When her husband qualified they left to live in Damascus.

Boris introduced me to some Kurds from whom he bought dollars. It was refreshing to meet men who did not consider falling unconscious to the floor the apotheosis of a good time. We went out to celebrate Syrian Independence day. The Kurds played folk music, Russian students performed Cossack dances, and a Syrian recited Pushkin very beautifully. Afterwards everyone sat down to cakes and warm champagne. While Russian women drank and danced with the foreigners, the Russian men behaved like their British counterparts in Mediterranean discotheques. They skulked together in a dark corner, paralysing themselves with vodka.

There is an almost Oriental degree of sex segregation in Samara. Women generally mix with women, apart from their male relations. The importance of female relationships was emphasised by one woman who came to me for English lessons. Married to a flourishing *biznesman*, she had decided to give up her job, for it was all she could do to run the household and care for her son. It seemed insane to work for a monthly salary which her husband could earn in a day. My student said her female colleagues had been horrified. They asked her what she would do with her time. For whom would she dress up? They thought she was renouncing her social life and retreating from the world, such is the importance of work as an escape from the confines of the home. As with so many women, her work collective has constituted her social life, and she was starting to grow lonely spending her whole day at home.

Whenever I was introduced to women older than myself their first question was whether or not I was married. They would utter the single Russian word *zamuzhem?* in a hiss of eager curiosity. My answer in the negative always produced a frisson of excitement as they ran a list of potential suitors through their brains. They would then ask in a tone of sly intimacy, "Would you consider a nice Russian man?"

My eventual liaison with a nice and relatively sober Russian man really taught me about life on the inside. I was no longer the foreign observer but potentially "one of us." After Slava and I had been spotted together in the market a few times news spread around town. Older women I scarcely knew would conspiratorially pull me aside to ask when the wedding was going to take place.

Despite the levelling of the sex imbalance men are still treated as a precious commodity, reminding me of the women in the supermarket fighting over frozen pullets. Apparently I had entered the fray without realising it and seized a prize. The other women closed around me in a conspiracy to protect and care for this male as though he were a member of an endangered species.

A neighbour gave me advice on how to wash Slava's shirts. Dumbstruck, I could not bear to disillusion her with the truth. I had already shocked her to the core by saying I paid my own rent and bought my own food.

"That's not right dear, let him do that for you."

My greatest problem was how to deal with Slava's mother. A cheerful, kind-hearted soul, she turned into my inquisitor.

At first I enjoyed her visits, but gradually came to dread the doorbell. She used to call almost every day on her way home from work. Puffing and sweating from the effort of climbing my stairs with her shopping she would plump herself at the kitchen table while I made tea. Out of her bags came half-rotten vegetables or scraps of meat filched from the shop where she worked. Her eyes would roam searchingly over the kitchen as she asked what I was cooking that evening. Once she presented me with a bagful of bloody bones with which I was supposed to make her little boy a delicious stew. The stray dogs in the courtyard had a feast that evening. Did I have bread and sausage? I gambled on whether to lie or not because she was quite capable of opening my fridge to check on its contents.

When I finally told her that her son dined in his works canteen she was shocked into silence. Then her lips compressed in disapproval:

"I'll come around after work to cook his supper here," she announced.

A cultural abyss yawned before me. I was rooted to my side of the divide, but loath to hurt her feelings. When I told Slava to discourage his mother's offers of assistance he looked surprised:

"You didn't tell her you don't cook for me?"

"I didn't realise I was supposed to."

"But of course she wants to come round to make sure I am alright."

Female friends laughed in sympathy. The wife of a former army officer said, "My husband is forty years old but his mother still comes by every evening with a dish of dumplings she has baked for her little boy."

Soon enough, I learned that it is impossible to form relations with men without one's intentions being misconstrued.

One day Slava called and introduced me to an old acquaintance of his. This man was an Afghan veteran, a member of the elite Blue Berets. Shattered by his war experiences, he was selling his flat and emigrating to Germany where he had relatives. He drove us out to a "sought-after" residential area.

As he showed us around his flat a dreadful suspicion took hold of me. Outside, Slava confirmed my fears:

"I can arrange a bank loan to buy this flat. I thought we might get married. We wouldn't be badly off. You would be able to eat oranges every day. As you don't like housework mother can move in and look after us."

I returned this 30 year old man to his mother, who was far more devoted to him than I could ever be. Thus I learned that a woman who wants male company is supposed to marry one.

When Ivan the Terrible was under pressure from rebellious boyars he made plans to flee abroad. He asked Elizabeth the First of England for asylum, which she promised him. Thus encouraged, he offered to marry her. Wisely, she ignored his proposal. I decided to take a leaf out of her book and turn a deaf ear to all future advances.

Provincial Russian society makes it hard for those women who do not conform. Single women are objects of pity or fear. Many women stay in their unhappy marriages because they equate solitude with loneliness. Yet divorce is much easier to obtain in Russia than it is in Britain; the hard part is finding separate accommodation. It is impossible for someone to go home to mother if she is already living with them.

After the revolution there were experiments with different types of relationship. Divorce was a simple procedure that took place outside the courts. Living arrangements were reorganised with the aim of communalising home and child care, although the idea of domestic work as the female's responsibility was never challenged. Number Four, Specialist Alley was the legacy of revolutionary experimentation: in the communal kitchen each woman toiled under the eyes of her neighbours.

By 1926 the family had been restored as a unit of social control of the individual, playing a fundamental role in the maintenance of Soviet society. Propaganda was mixed with indirect methods of compulsion. The exhortation to raise a "healthy Soviet family" justified close scrutiny of personal life. It was vital for both men and women to show "stable moral behaviour" as family members. Whatever went on behind the scenes, appearances had to be maintained. Little has changed to this day.

In 1988 a London cinema premiered the Russian film *Lonely Woman Seeks Life Partner.* Afterwards, the male director came on stage for a discussion. British women in the audience could not understand the point of the film. Why had the 40 year old heroine, with a good job and comfortable flat, wanted to take in a drunkard who had been kicked out by his wife? They suspected the director of trying to undermine the concept of female autonomy. He looked bemused, shrugged, and replied, "Because it is sad to live alone."

Life in Samara convinced me that the director was attempting nothing more sinister than a portrayal of prevalent Russian attitudes. Almost without exception, women would rather live with a man, however alcoholic and abusive, than live independently. For their part, men latch onto females much as a dissolute English lord might have put himself in the hands of his valet. Within this symbiotic relationship the wife may have firm control over domestic life, yet her social status is determined by the fact that she serves the man.

At heart Russian women see men as helpless boobies. This realisation hit me during a discussion with Valentina on homosexuality: "If you have so many homosexuals in the West it is because you women have made them that way. What with lesbianism and feminism the poor things have no idea how to treat a woman."

The other women present nodded in agreement. Most women saw homosexuality as a problem (even when they idolised Freddie Mercury). Their hostility may have arisen from resentment or fear that homosexuality was shrinking the pool of eligible men.

Female impetus to govern male behaviour is so overwhelming that they seem incapable of seeing men as autonomous individuals. Wives will argue with husbands and then ring their mothers-in-law to ask them to instill some sense in their sons.

This syndrome has led some writers such as Tatiana Tolstaya to conclude that Russia is a matriarchal society. This is the equivalent of arguing that workers control an economy, because it could not function without them. In practice men hold economic and political power in Russia; women give them the support which enables them to wield it.

Years ago a Russian émigré shocked me by claiming her sex counted for nothing in the Soviet Union. In those days I was still swayed by images of female astronauts and tractor drivers. After living in Samara I realised that émigré had been right. Although no stranger to female servility, I was shocked by the lowly status of Russian women. Millions of intelligent and extremely capable women are convinced they need a man to protect them because they count for nothing. In order to count for something they make themselves indispensable to others.

Russian women exude boundless competence. Although often thankful to find myself in their all-embracing care, I sometimes felt as though I was being treated as an honourary man or an invalid. I reflected that if I were a man I would rather have a friend than a nursemaid. There again, if I were a Russian man the chances are I would find the contents of a bottle more compelling than female company.

The post-war Soviet Union was a modern, industrialised society. If it could put women into space it could have built efficient public laundries on every block. One of the reasons it did not do so was that it expected women to continue to be the caryatids of the economy and the home. Most depressing of all, they expect it of themselves.

The architects of post-communist shock therapy risked catastrophic austerity measures. If British employers withheld wages for months in the face of hyperinflation, if dole and pensions were reduced to 10 pounds a week, then civil disturbances would break out all over the country. In Russia however, the brunt of the shock has been absorbed by women. As long as they have land to cultivate and a supply of saleable goods they strive to maintain a semblance of normality, wearing themselves out in the process. The spectre of the women bread rioters who triggered the 1917 revolution seems very remote.

Escaping the Collective Farm

"Most of the buildings are wooden . . . after rainfall, mud renders the streets almost impassable, and in dry weather dust clouds blind the eyes and choke the breath. One day shortly after my arrival, a veritable tornado whipped up so much dust that for several minutes I could not even see the buildings on the other side of the street. Amongst these primitive surroundings the colossal new church seems inappropriate; looking at it, the thought occurred to me that some of the money spent on its construction might have been used in a more productive manner."

The Scottish traveller Donald Mackenzie Wallace's
view of Samara in the 1870s.

Today a giant Stalinist opera house stands in place of Samara's cathedral. After the revolution all but three of the city's 50 churches were razed to the ground. The city centre is now paved, although drains are still unable to cope with the spring rains. Outlying settlements, however, still look much as they would have in Mackenzie Wallace's time. In the effort to industrialize, the countryside was bled by the state as it once was by the church. Infrastructure in the country was neglected; roads still turn into a sea of mud in spring, and in summer the villages are covered in dust.

Country life is grim. In the 1930s Stalin forcibly collectivized land into *kolkhozes* and *sovkhozes* (collective farms and larger state farms). Internal passports were issued to all Soviet citizens except collective farm workers, preventing them from leaving the land and effectively reducing them to serfdom. Agriculture was the weakest sector in the Soviet economy. Today the privatisation of farmland is slow. Lack of credit and a poor rural infrastructure have made farmers reluctant to lease land from collectives.

Valentina, the refugee in London who arranged my invitation to Samara, had been born and brought up on the *Oktyabr sovkhoz* outside the city. Valentina had two younger sisters, Kira and Sveta. Each had found her own way to escape the farm. Kira went to work on the railways as a *provodnitsa*, Sveta married and moved to the city and Valentina emigrated to Germany. Later she made her way to London. When she came back on a two-week visit to Russia she took me down to the *Oktyabr Sovkhoz*, but was in a bad temper when she called for me.

"I only arrived yesterday and want to leave already. I had forgotten how barbaric our everyday life is. Imagine, the shop assistant refused to wrap up my eggs. I told her that people in civilized countries do not accept such low standards of service."

As for me, I always meekly accepted my unwrapped eggs and was pleased if even seven out of ten survived the packed tram ride home. I must have adapted to Russian life more quickly than I realised.

On that hot August morning Valentina's uncle fetched us from the city and drove us down to the *sovkhoz*. A film of dust coated the farm; it was ingrained in the creases of our driver's neck. A couple of *babushki* sat on a bench outside the block where Valentina's parents lived. When we said good morning they continued to stare impassively into the distance.

I suppose like most city people I had been expecting some rustic idyll. I loved the untamed countryside along the banks of the Volga, where I felt as though I were stepping through the pages of Turgenev. But the *sovkhoz* had turned exuberant nature into business—not very successfully. It was a desolate and forlorn place. Externally it reminded me of a Hudson Bay Indian reservation I once visited, but it fostered even more drunkenness and decay.

Ten thousand people lived in scattered settlements of concrete three-storey flats. Between these snaked a jumble of raised water and gas pipes. The *sovkhoz* had an almost empty general store, and a bookshop selling dusty communist literature and children's books. The Marlboro revolution had passed the farm by; Bulgarian cigarettes were all it had to offer. *Sovkhozniki* without their own transport had to walk to the main road and catch the bus to Samara to do their shopping. They had a recreation room where dances were sometimes held, but hard drinking was their main distraction from rural life.

Valentina's mother flung open her door and welcomed us with tears and signs of the cross. Her father shuffled out of the inner room to kiss us and then retreated. An alcoholic, he no longer worked. Occasionally he escaped the flat for a drinking session. He had became so uncontrollable after a recent bout that his wife sent him to a psychiatric hospital to dry out for a few weeks.

While Valentina and her sister Kira prepared breakfast their mother took me out onto the balcony. The air reeked of manure. Below us chickens grubbed in the dirt. Cabbages and sunflowers grew on a private patch of land. These formed the mother's livelihood, supplementing her basic pension. Thrice weekly she travelled to Samara to sell her vegetables, eggs, and sunflower oil in the market. The other *sovkhozniki* spent as much time as they could on their own private plots. Their produce was in demand in the city for the state shops were filling up with inferior packaged foodstuffs imported from the West. Townspeople who could afford it preferred to buy fresh vegetables and cheese in the farmers' market.

The girls laid salad, chicken, beer, vodka and pink champagne on the table. Valentina showed off photos of herself having Christmas dinner in London. Her mother pored over the pictures with greedy fascination, asking what each bottle and dish contained. She could no more imagine English life than she could another colour, but food on the table held a tangible meaning. She studied a photo of Waterloo station—"Does it have kiosks selling chocolate and liqueurs like those on Samara's central station?"

The morning sun had heated up the flat like an oven. I felt faint in the stifling living room and begged Kira to open a window. She warned that flies would come in from the chicken run outside. Too groggy for politeness, I insisted. Almost as soon as she opened the balcony door the food and champagne glasses became encrusted with a heaving black swarm. I felt sick. Kira suggested we go to bathe in the lake and packed up a crate of beer to take with us. We trooped out past the silent *babushki*.

The dirt track to the lake ran alongside wooden cattle sheds. Valentina held her nose and hurried past them as though she was a stranger to their smell. Trucks and ancient motorbikes with sidecars roared by, choking us with dust clouds. The lake turned out to be a large muddy watering-hole for cattle. We lay on the trodden earth by the water's edge, fighting a losing battle against flies. To escape them we submerged ourselves in the pond. Scrawny blonde youths gathered on the bank to stare as we wallowed like hippos. I stared back and recalled pictures of thirties dust bowl America. It made me dizzy to think of this arid, undulating grassland spreading out around us for thousands of miles.

Kira was a taciturn girl with a masculine air. I saw with surprise that she wore no make up. I had grown used to the masks of city women who considered themselves naked if they left the house with unpainted lips and eyelids.

Kira said she had never intended to become a dairy maid or tractor driver. Not wanting her life circumscribed by the *sovkhoz*, she had found a job as a *provodnitsa* on the railways. Her route took her to a town on the Siberian river Ob. The journey there and back lasted six days. Then she had a few days off which allowed her to help her mother at home. Kira enjoyed her job. She met different people and was able to do some trading en route. She had paid a brief visit to Valentina in England but had not been impressed. "All that glitters is not gold," was her only comment. I thought she was the most sensible of the three sisters.

The second sister, Sveta, had won a place at Samara's prestigious medical school. There she had opportunely fallen in love with a fellow student. She had tried her hardest to persuade Pavel to marry her but he was not interested. He and his family had set their sights higher than an alliance with a *sovkhoz* girl without connections. Pavel had well-off parents. His father, a chief engineer in a meat processing plant, had made a lot of money by selling sausages through the back door to the highest bidder, bribing the plant's accountants and stock-takers to cover his tracks.

Sveta got pregnant and refused to have an abortion. Pavel finally agreed to marry her provided the child was kept on the *sovkhoz* where her mother would look after it. Thus Sveta realised her dream and moved into a flat with Pavel in the city centre, in an area where "professionals" live, she told me proudly. The couple showed an interest in me as a foreigner and friend of Valentina's, inviting me to their flat a few times. By local standards they were extremely well off. Pavel's father had provided them with a two-room flat, a car, and a small motor-launch on the river. That spring they had travelled abroad for the first time.

Since 1991 the residents of formerly closed cities have been allowed to travel abroad. All that is required is a large amount of hard currency. The local papers and TV stations advertise a selection of package-tour destinations. The most popular are Turkey and the UAE, where a week costs from 400 to 600 dollars. These shopping excursions are mainly for cheap electronic goods which are then resold for a profit in Russia.

Pavel and Sveta had spent a week in Istanbul. Although the city had made little impression on them, they were eager to show off the camcorder and video they had bought. I spent a boring evening trying to translate instructions that I barely understood myself. Then I was subjected to a video of their white wedding in the city's brutalist-style Palace of Marriages. "My husband's death," beamed Sveta.

She waited on him hand and foot, apologising if a dish was not quite to his liking. He spoke to her as though she were his servant. I once asked her why it was necessary to do all the housework, considering that she also had a job in a clinic. "But if I did not have his dinner ready on the table he might not come home."

In response to her husband's denigration Sveta insisted that she was a socially useful citizen. She justified her existence by working in a newly opened private beauty clinic. In this grisly salon women paid two months' salary to have the skin chemically peeled off their faces. At present only mafia wives could afford the treatment. Face-lifting and cosmetic surgery were being promoted in the media. Sveta looked blank when I asked if she thought this was a good thing—"Of course. We need to attract more women to our clinic."

Sveta said she missed her two-year old daughter, whom she visited every week or so. She was one of the few women in Samara who could drive, but in spring Pavel would not let her use the car in case it was dirtied by the muddy roads.

I wondered if in her more lucid moments Sveta doubted the worth of trading the dust, flies and boredom of the farm for her present life of domestic servitude. But she would never have considered her situation in those terms. She did not see herself as a slave. Household drudgery would have played a large part in whatever life she chose. I am sure she congratulated herself every time she drove away from the *sovkhoz* back to her shiny new city flat.

Valentina had planned her escape over several years. A bright woman, she had been accepted into Samara's university to read mathematics. She had also been active in the *Komsomol*, in the hope of qualifying for the privilege of foreign travel. In 1989 she was given permission to visit Germany, where she claimed political asylum. Before that she had been making plans to move to Moscow after graduation, but when she reached the West "her eyes were opened," as she put it, and she defected. She was put in a refugee hostel while the authorities considered her case.

"The hostel was a madhouse. By day I would escape and walk around the streets. I knew every mansion in the Wannsee. I used to stand at the gates and dream I owned those houses. Sometimes I walked along the Kurfurstendamm crying at the sight of all the beautiful clothes I could never afford. I could not believe that I had lived 30 years of my life without even imagining such things.

"I married a German and gained EC status. Last year we came to England as you have a better social security system. I think the English are highly considerate and respectful of each other in public, but underneath you don't give a damn about anyone."

Valentina was wildly naïve about the workings of capitalism. She fell for every marketing ploy, trying pyramid selling and answering all magazine ads for "free gifts." She was once lured onto a timeshare induction course by the announcement that she had won a holiday in Miami. Lack of a valid passport scuppered that project. She pursues the capitalist dream with obsessive force, voting Conservative and proclaiming, oddly, that "England should be for the English." Convinced that happiness is dependent on external trappings, she channels her intelligence and energy into the pursuit of material wealth. Each new acquisition gives her fleeting pleasure. She holds soirées to show off her clothes and furniture to her friends, then sets herself back on the treadmill to toil for the next object of desire. Back in London she could not even bear to look at photos of Samara, saying she did not want to be reminded of her days on the edge of civilisation. Having seen her background I realised she was trying to erect a safety barrier of possessions, as though her *Estée Lauder* foundation and *Next* suit could protect her from the attendant unpleasantness of poverty.

It is hard to say what quirk of personality will prompt one person to fight against a situation while another will tolerate it. The three sisters on the *sovkhoz* had been aware of their position at the bottom of the social pile. They knew the only way out, apart from the bottle, was up.

As the sun dipped over the horizon we left the pond and trooped back to the flat. The stony *babushki* were still sitting on their bench, immobile and uncomprehending. It was unlikely that these old ladies had ever been farther than the city of Samara in their lives. In their youth, Valentina's grandmothers had not been allowed to leave the farm.

That evening our return bus broke down half-way and we had to hitch the remaining 20 kilometres. Valentina said this was a common occurrence. The transport system is wearing out due to lack of investment. While the more profitable intercity rail network still functions efficiently, the ancient country buses turn to scrap.

By the standards of many farms the *Oktyabr sovkhoz* was a good one. It was near a city, giving the *sovkhozniki* access to markets, shops, hospitals and colleges. Its ugly flats had internal sanitation, gas and electricity. The old Russian rural houses may look charming but they usually lack internal plumbing. This means women have to fetch and carry water in all weathers. The more remote farms are reached by unmetalled roads, which turn to mud in spring and autumn, isolating the communities.

In agriculture, as in every other sector of the Russian economy, the hardest jobs fall to women. Khrushchev once remarked that "It is the men who do the administration and the women who do the work."[7] When a process is mechanised men usually take over. Although the proportion of women in skilled positions has risen since the 1950s they are still concentrated in the lowly jobs of crop-picking, weeding and dairying. The latter is a time-consuming process that can stretch over 18 hours of a day with only short breaks in between milking. Dairymaids work for years on end without being granted a day off, only

---

[7] *Izvestiya*, 26 Dec 1961, p. 4.

winning release if they can find someone to cover for them. Tractor driving is considered a lighter occupation than dairying and is therefore dominated by men. Government campaigns to train female tractor drivers faced concerted male opposition.

World war two left an even greater sex imbalance in the countryside than in the towns. Throughout the fifties and sixties men poured away from the farms, the surest route being through military service, when passports were temporarily returned to their holders. Once they left the army young men seized the opportunity to find work in factories. When passports were granted to all peasants in 1975 women began to vote with their feet, creating a situation called the "the bride problem." As droves of young women left in search of a better life young men followed, for there was almost no one left to marry in the villages. Only the old remained in the countryside.

At present the exodus from country to town has slowed. There is little work in Samara apart from street-trading. Defence plants are closing. The future is so uncertain that some city dwellers talk of returning to the land. A couple of unemployed factory workers told me they planned to move out to their grandmother's house in the country.

"We used to say Granny lived in a village without a future. Like so many in Russia, it would die with the last of its old people. Now we would like to move back to grow vegetables and keep pigs, hens and bees. But we are afraid of banditry. God knows where the robbers come from, but if they scent a whiff of prosperity they break into the farms. Cars and goods vans drive in convoy along country roads out there."

In Russia there is a stark division between town and country. Urban dwellers tend to view village life with horror. An English-language lecturer who lived in one of the rooms in

Specialist Alley said that when she graduated from teacher training college she had been ordered out to work in a distant village.

"As there was an excess of English graduates I was sent out to the back of beyond. I might as well have been on the moon. There was no point of contact between myself and the peasants. But I was obliged to repay the state for my education. Although married, my husband was only a student and we were not permitted to live together. I was allowed back to the city to stay with him for two weeks in the year. After a few months I resolved the situation by getting pregnant. Only then could I leave that godforsaken village and return to Samara. We were allocated this room in which we still live with our grown-up daughter."

A political exile from Moscow who was sent to work on a Siberian *kolkhoz* in the seventies wrote that the collective farms would never work properly until the kolkhozniki learned to respect themselves:

"Just as the *kolkhoznik* knows he is not allowed to leave the farm, so he also knows he will not be expelled however badly he works."[8]

When this urban, educated man tried to argue with a visiting Party official the peasants rounded on him in horror. They might break the rules on the sly, grease palms and get drunk on the job, but open dissent was inconceivable. The exile concluded that the farm's inhabitants were "People with whom you can do anything."[9]

Although not long removed from the country themselves,

---

[8] Andrei Amalrik, Involuntary Journey to Siberia (Collins and Harvill press, for the Readers Union, Newton Abbot, 1971) p. 168.
[9] ibid.

many urban Samarans believed they were a race apart. Whenever I mentioned the number of drunks on the streets or aggression on public transport, townspeople laid the blame on boorish peasants who had only just moved into the city and had not yet learned how to behave. One language teacher sighed in an exaggerated posture of suffering and said "You see how I, an educated person, am tormented by this rabble on the streets and in the markets. They are building all these new *micro-raioni* and filling them up with *sovkhozniki*."

I felt this was unfair, yet in Samara I indulged in my own form of snobbery. The materialism and provincial small-mindedness of many—by no means all—Samarans got me down. I grew tired of being asked how much *Snickers* bars cost in Britain and whether I had seen the lovely prizes won on last night's TV game show. To counteract this I had to remind myself that Moscow and London are as capable of producing such attitudes as Samara or a *sovkhoz*. Equally, as I had seen, the *sovkhoz* could produce bold and independent spirits.

But as for having to live on a Russian farm—it would be one of the last places on earth I would choose.

The *Babushka* Economy

"I've had enough of him, the boozer!" ranted the old man. "He took my trousers, he stole my white stallion. It cost 179 roubles in Moscow."

Through the open door I saw a colonel look up in surprise from his desk. His troubled eyes met mine. Between us a bent old man leaned heavily on his stick. The colonel obviously wanted to rid himself of this lunatic with three rows of medals on his chest but was loath to offend a hero of the Great Patriotic War. Then his face cleared in relief.

"You mean a toy horse?"

"Yes, yes. He took it and sold it for vodka. I want my son evicted from my flat."

Just then the beetle-like woman who always dealt with my *propiska* scuttled up and ushered me into her office. In an unprecedented display of humanity she confided "This happens all the time. Pensioners mistake these offices for the police station opposite. As soon as they see a uniform they think of someone to denounce."

Veterans of the second world war still enjoy privileges. They pay only 50% of their domestic bills, receive free medicine and bus passes and take priority in queues. Housewives say they cannot not help resenting veterans who walked past them as they stand exhausted in queues, although they respect the old and think the Western practice of putting aged parents in homes barbaric.

There are far more old women than old men. The war created a heavy sex imbalance and women outlive men by an average of ten years, being somewhat less prone to alcoholism and related accidents. And it is older women who carry Russia on their backs. Theirs are the heaviest, dirtiest, most poorly-paid tasks. They sweep streets, clean toilets, weed the fields and maintain railway tracks. Retirement does not mean they stop work. Inflation has eroded the basic pension to virtually nothing, so most continue to work in the unofficial economy. An ancient lady cleaned my local police station for the equivalent of a dollar a month. Others combed the streets for discarded bottles to return for a few roubles. Aged beggars cluster around churches in scenes of pre-revolution squalor.

It is taken for granted that grandmothers will serve as baby-sitters, freeing younger women to go out to work. They also queue for the family's food. The longest queue in town is outside the state-run vodka shop. Pensioners are either paid to keep someone's place in the line, or they stock up on bottles to resell back in their *micro-raioni*.

Babushki with dachas sell their produce by the roadside, placing a few apples or carrots, perhaps a bunch of dahlias and a jar of pickles on an upturned crate. They sit awaiting customers for 12 to 14 hours a day, summer and winter. Periodically the police sweep them away from their pitches, but they always return the following day.

Boris's mother Nina Alexandrovna was one of the vast *babushka* army of super-exploited labour. Her job was extremely hard and badly-paid. Exhausted, she asked for early retirement and was threatened with confinement in a psychiatric hospital. She was utterly defenceless, cowed by authority and had no idea of her rights. I have never met anyone with such low expectations of life. Boris said she was unexceptional; simply a product of Stalinism.

Nina was born in Leningrad. Her parents were killed by a German bomb at the start of the war. She was pulled alive from the rubble of their house and sent away to a children's home in Samara. At school she showed exceptional talent as a gymnast and was recruited into the local circus as an acrobat. When they went on tour she returned to the city of her birth. She transferred to the Leningrad State circus where she worked as a trapeze artist for seven years.

Nina said that if she had stayed with the circus she would be retired by now and have her own flat and *dacha*. She had to leave when she married and became pregnant, so she returned to Samara, where Boris was born. The husband proved to be an alcoholic and Nina left him. Unfortunately she had nowhere to live except a hostel which had no provision for children. She had to put Boris in a children's home and wait seven years before they were allocated a room in a communal flat on the edge of town.

I first met Nina at her workplace in the basement kitchens of the Ministry of Railways. In her white headscarf and overalls she looked like a shock worker from a Stalinist poster. I invited her home to tea. As we emerged from the building we were besieged by stray cats, pigeons and sparrows. Nina threw them stale bread and cake that she had filched from the kitchens.

"They wait for me every day. They know the time I leave work."

Nina prattled like a very young child. Her thoughts tumbled out, interrupted by bursts of laughter at her own jokes. Sometimes she forgot simple words such as "biscuit." I realised she had never been in the habit of conversing with anyone.

We reached Boris's room and Nina complained of tiredness and a headache. I offered an aspirin but she smiled, shook her head and suddenly turned a handstand on the floor. Then she lay down, tucked one foot behind her shoulder, leaped up again, and stood on her head in a corner. Finally she sprang to her feet and bowed to an imaginary audience. At 55 Nina was as supple as a teenager.

The collective who ran the dining room at the Ministry of Railways were mostly Party members. Apart from the kitchen porters, they were all women. Nina said she felt like a "white raven" amongst the collective because she did not drink.

"Why do people drink? They always bring vodka into work. I hear them laughing together when they're drinking. But we sit here and laugh without vodka."

The others were suspicious of her because of this, and had accused her of being a drug addict and a Baptist. She said they would drink all day, on any pretext. They also teased her about me, saying that someone like her could not possibly know an Englishwoman and that she was only trying to make herself sound important by claiming that she did.

Nina rose at five in the morning and travelled to work in a packed and often unheated bus. The journey took an hour and she often arrived chilled to the bone. She toiled for seven hours without a break in the damp basement below the railway offices. She reached home exhausted. The collective filched bagfuls of food from the kitchens, leaving her with a few buns and half-rotten potatoes as perks of the job. For this gruelling labour Nina was paid 15,000 roubles a month (about 15 dollars). A factory worker could expect 30,000 to 100,000 a month. People with "dirty jobs" like Nina's have to give two months' notice before they can leave their positions, and then stay on until the employers find a replacement.

While Boris lived in the city centre to be near his work, Nina cared for his canary, parakeet and lazy white Persian cat in their one-room flat in an industrial suburb. One day I was having tea with Boris when Nina called in tears. She had burnt her leg in the kitchens. The wound was infected and oozing pus. She had asked her boss for time off to see a doctor but was told her pay would be docked. Boris explained her rights and slipped her a bank note.

"Take a taxi home, see the doctor tomorrow, and take as much time off as you want."

Drying her tears, she looked up at him in adoration: "You used to be so tiny and now you've grown so big."

A week later we went over to see how she was. Boris pulled me into the kitchen: "Look, she hasn't touched the fruit and honey I brought her." He opened the fridge. It contained tins of salmon, shrimp and caviare. There was a chicken in the ice compartment.

"It's all for the cat. She never eats that sort of food herself. That's what she did with the money I gave her. She did not even take a taxi home the day she hurt her leg. It never occurs to her to look after herself."

But she had spent the remainder of the money on a pair of black velvet stilettoes.

"For the theatre," she explained.

"Which you attend every night," said an exasperated Boris.

He told me later "That's why I don't give her a lot of money all at once. Her wardrobe is stuffed with shoes, dresses and jewellery that she never wears. She never goes out in the evening, of course."

I sympathised with her efforts to brighten her life with sparkly adornments. She still dyed her hair platinum blonde and painted her eyebrows in Dietrich arcs. The next time we visited Nina she flew into a temper: "Why can't I have a TV set? Do we live in the stone age? I've been off work for two weeks now and I'm bored sitting up here all day."

Nina had no idea that a small set cost half a million roubles, which represented three years' wages for her. She saw it as a pretty toy. I had seen her sit for hours in front of Boris' set, intently following the pictures with the sound turned down. Sometimes she would take a pencil and sketch a dress that took her fancy in an old Soviet film. Then she would spin dreams of having it made up by the local dressmaker.

Nina and her son reflected the difference between the Stalin and perestroika generations. Boris often remarked that his mother displayed the "mentality of poverty," yet it was painfully apparent that his own world view was shaped by the deprivation of his youth. He pictured himself marching steadily towards material success, with a sound system, TV, video, and car as milestones along the way.

Russians are now bombarded with evidence of what money could buy if only they had it. Consumer goods are the carrots on sticks that encourage conformity to society's new values. For millions like Boris the lack of possessions is a sign of backwardness and personal failure.

He once gave me a CD of Rachmaninov concertos. I was touched, but explained I had nothing to play it on.

"I thought everyone in the West had a CD player," he said in genuine surprise.

Nina, on the other hand, had been brought up in poverty in a non-consumerist society. Straightforward fear of authority had instilled obedience in her. From early childhood she had been taught that she was of no significance at all. She had enjoyed a few years of glory in the circus, and then sunk to obscurity. She was unusual in that she had developed a taste for spangles and diamanté. Otherwise she was unable to make any correlation between "luxury goods" and herself. If Boris ever makes his fortune Nina will feed the cat caviare off a silver spoon while continuing to live on black bread, pickled cabbage, and rotten potatoes.

Like most Russian mothers, Nina saw herself as her son's personal servant. Arriving from a long journey one afternoon, Boris and I fell asleep in her flat. For four days the water supply to the block had been turned off for the usual "technical reasons." While we slept Nina trudged down to the pump in the street and carried buckets of water back up five flights of stairs. I awoke, embarrassed. Boris offered to fetch more water but Nina said she had enough and went into the kitchen to cook supper. She expected nothing from her son except money.

Nina also suffered from a blood disorder exacerbated by her heavy manual job. At work she had attacks of dizziness, faintness, and was sometimes unable to stand up. She was examined by a doctor who diagnosed depression and neurasthenia. The report read:

"Nina Alexandrovna says she 'does not want to work,' and 'does not want to do anything' despite the results of tests which indicate normal health."

The doctor told Nina that she would be sent to a psychiatric hospital. "They will pinch you there, shout at you, shave your head, but don't take any notice, it will be good for you to go in. You will be able to have a rest."

Her employers were looking for an excuse to sack her without compensation. It was illegal to dismiss her for reasons of physical health, and if it could be proved that her ill health was due to poor work conditions they would have to pay compensation.

When he heard about the Ministry of Railways' plan to send his mother to a psychiatric hospital Boris stepped in. He told her to leave her job and tended her himself, giving her ten thousand roubles a week to buy what she needed.

I asked Nina if she had any friends.

"I met a porter at work. We got along well and he asked me to live with him. Unfortunately he drank, so after six months I left him. Now I do not mix with anyone, it only leads to trouble. I learned that in the children's home. My neighbours are all drunks. I greet them and that is all. It is dangerous to go out in this area after dark. Yesterday evening I was standing in the bread queue and a couple of young girls started jeering at me. They were laughing so unnaturally I guessed they had been taking drugs. What do I do all day? Housework. There is always something to be washed or cleaned."

When Boris is not around Nina talks to her animals. Like Lina Ivanovna, she is happy in the companionship of her menagerie. I thought how sensible these women were to have foregone the opportunity of slaving for drunken husbands. It was easy to see how the legions of so-called witches throughout history might have preferred the company of animals to people.

Russians often refer to someone approvingly as *prostoi*, meaning they are down-to-earth and lacking in sophistication. Nina Alexandrovna was extremely *prostaya* and dignified. Once when we were hurrying for a tram a man tried to push her aside: "Out of my way, Granny, you're holding me up."

"I am not 'Granny,'" she replied, "My name is Nina Alexandrovna, and I have hurt my leg."

Nina's horizons were bounded by the walls of her home and the slimy catacombs of her workplace. She would happily tell me about the little birds that sang on her balcony in the morning sun, but she never asked me about England. From fragments of chatter I gathered that she imagined it to be like Russia, except safer and with more goods in the shops.

There is a tendency amongst the Russian intelligentsia to eulogise "our simple Russian people" yet the Tsarist and Soviet systems were based on the exploitation of people like Nina Alexandrovna. Perhaps her kind are dying out. The younger women I met were less prepared to accept slave labour, at least where their official jobs were concerned.

My next-door neighbour at Number Four also belonged to the ranks of the super-exploited, although she had more cunning than Nina. Baba Tonya lived with her alcoholic husband and seven cats. She had been born in the building 67 years ago. Her mother died when she was three and her father, an alcoholic, was killed at the front when she was 15. For 38 years she worked as a quality controller at the *Victory* watch factory. She had been a model worker and when she retired ten years ago had expected to be allocated her own flat. She did not receive one and still cries over her disappointment.

As a young woman she had broken her back by falling downstairs. She lay in hospital for three years. Now she walks with a limp. Her spine is curved and her neck twisted. She is also diabetic. Despite her health problems, the authorities refuse to give her a flat. She lacks the connections to help them change their minds. Baba Tonya now expects to die in the building where she was born.

In late 1993 she was receiving a pension of 18,000 roubles a month. After rent and electricity had been paid this bought a loaf of bread and a litre of milk a day. Her husband, Grandad Kostya, had a portering job, but he spent every last rouble of his wages on drink. Sometimes when he came in after a night shift he would collapse in the corridor, too drunk to reach his room. Baba Tonya would drag him in as best she could, treating the other residents of the flat to a torrent of obscenities as she struggled to put him to bed. We all pretended not to hear these tirades, because they contradicted the sweet old lady image she tried so hard to project as her means of survival.

Baba Tonya supplemented her pension by street trading, but the back injury made it excruciatingly painful to stand out in the cold for long. Boris came to the rescue by paying her to cook and clean for him.

When I asked Baba Tonya where I should dump my household rubbish she told me to leave it outside my door. The next day she returned the plastic rubbish sack, carefully washed and dried. A few days later she brought back a pair of threadbare old socks I had thrown away. She had found them while picking through my rubbish, washed and mended them. "Don't throw good things away." Chastened, I never again threw out any polythene bag, glass jar or rag that might have been of use to Baba Tonya.

She knew she could get whatever she wanted out of Boris and me and probably the rest of her neighbours by putting on her little old lady act. She burst into tears at every opportunity. In the face of this we would give her whatever she had her eye on (British supermarket carrier bags in my case). Her delight in her own craftiness made her even more endearing.

Baba Tonya's greatest joy in life was the American TV soap *Santa Barbara*. The rich of California were too remote to elicit her envy, but her aspirations extended to *Whiskas* cat food which she had seen advertised on television. A new import, small cans cost 1,200 roubles. Baba Tonya constantly fretted over her cats. Besides the seven hungry animals in her room, she fed the feral creatures who lived in nooks and crannies in the building. Consumerism was taking effect; she felt she was failing her darlings by not giving them what she was told was the best.

The government's intention to triple the price of electricity was an ominous threat to Baba Tonya. She and her husband were too young to qualify for veterans' allowances. She cried every time she thought of the future.

Baba Tonya's greatest friend lived in the flat above ours. Nina Mikhailovna was a retired *provodnitsa*.

"I retired after they cut off my breast and then found nothing wrong with it. That's the way doctors operated four or five years ago. They cut off bits of your body first before deciding you did not have cancer.

"I worked as a *provodnitsa* for ten years. I used to travel up to Estonia and back. They are good-looking people up there, except the men, who have the eyes of dying fish washed up on the beach.

"We were a good crew. The boys who ran the restaurant car were the cleanest people you could meet. They were homosexual and used to get up to all kinds of hanky-panky.

"Homosexuality was not even discussed until recently; under socialism they pretended it did not exist. Baba Tonya says she never heard of such a thing until she was 40."

Nina Mikhailovna was a breath of fresh air blowing through the stuffy bigotry of Samaran society. I liked all three women I knew who had been *provodnitsi*: Nina, Kira and Lina Ivanovna. Perhaps travel had opened their eyes beyond the limited horizons of the average citizen, or perhaps the work simply attracted more broad-minded and adventurous women.

Nina and Baba Tonya were an endearing sight. Nina would stride forth with her grey hair flying, her one breast bouncing in her overalls, with Baba Tonya limping along behind, trying to compose her features into an expression of martyred benevolence. Whenever I saw them together I guessed they had hatched some money-making scheme. One day they approached me with a business proposition:

"How much do those pretty little bags cost in England?"

"Well, nothing really. You are given them when you buy something from a supermarket."

The two could barely contain their excitement.

"Next time you come here bring 1,000 with you. It is stupid for you to travel empty-handed. You might as well cover the cost of your trip. We will take those bags down to the market and sell them for you. Could you possibly find some with naked girls on them?"

The old have supposedly been helped by humanitarian aid from the West. They joke bitterly over this, for most "aid" has been syphoned off by the mafia. A pilot who flew aid planes in from Denmark estimated about 30% of his cargo reached children's homes and church charity organisations. The rest fell into private hands. Horror stories abound. It was said that a local church received a consignment of German dog food and it was two weeks before someone translated the labels on the tins.

Life is easier for pensioners who have their own plots of land, which at least assure them of a food supply. I spent a weekend with a friend's aunt who lived in a private sector on the edge of the city. Auntie Nadya had a three-room cottage surrounded by a vegetable garden, at the end of which stood a wooden bath house. After steaming and beating myself with birch leaves, and dining on Auntie Nadya's pies and pickles I wanted to be nowhere else in this world. She showed me around her little house, saying self-deprecatingly that she lived like a collective farm worker. In fact she had more living space than anyone I knew in Samara. Her home was simple and charming, devoid of the seventies motel-style furniture favoured by the urban middle classes.

For Auntie Nadya housework was a source of pride and self-esteem rather than drudgery. She cooked with genius. She said she used to work as a cook in a family house; the privileges of the *nomenklatura* extended to personal servants.

Auntie Nadya and her home are relics of a past age. The world beyond her garden fence is changing, for the area in which she lives is now coveted by the nouveaux riches. Gypsies, grown rich from trading in vodka and second-hand cars, are paying old people to move out of their wooden cottages. They then move their families into the little houses, which they gradually enclose within a three-storey brick edifice. Those gypsy mansions are the strangest houses I have ever seen. Gates, balconies, turrets and rooftops glisten with spikes and spirals of twisted metal, a mixture of Gaudi and the Moghuls.

City dwellers were characteristically prejudiced against the Gypsies. Boris had been horrified that I should venture out to such a "dangerous" suburb. Auntie Nadya said she got along well with her neighbours, but she thought it odd that they built such beautiful big houses and put no furniture in them.

There was no inter-generational tension in Auntie Nadya's home. She was constantly visited by her son, grandchildren and nieces and as she never voiced a political opinion family harmony was preserved. In other homes my presence often brought underlying conflict into the open. Glad of a fresh audience, grandparents would tell me about the halcyon days of Stalin when sausage was cheap and there was no street crime. Their children and grandchildren would roll their eyes and mutter with irritation while I mumbled something tactful about the war. Granny would then be packed off to the shops or to watch television so that apologies could be made for her conservatism. Although deeply cynical of the new democrats, the young wanted no return to hardline communism.

A young teacher complained of the naïveté of her elderly relations: "They have never learned to see through politicians' lies. Zhirinovsky promises free state dining-rooms for pensioners so they go out and vote for him," she said in disgust.

Pensioners, victims of inflation and fearful for their personal safety, form the bulk of Communist supporters today. They say that before perestroika they never worried about opening their doors to callers. Nowadays they are frequent victims of mindless crime—usually alcohol-related. A veteran in Specialist Alley was robbed by neighbours who knocked on his door, first checking that the family who lived opposite were out. Looking through his spy-hole, the old man recognised them as the couple who lived above him. As he opened the door they knocked him to the ground and ransacked his flat. The only thing they considered worth stealing was his watch, which they sold for vodka. The police found them at home in a drunken stupor.

In public, elderly people who have been traumatised by childhoods of bloodshed and deprivation display a fathomless *priterpelost*. Only in church do old ladies shed their humility and assume the moral authority to scold men in tracksuit bottoms and women with uncovered heads. I find the choir singing of the Orthodox service more soothing than opium, but I am deterred by the praetorian guards of *babushki* hissing over my clothing.

Some of today's pensioners were born during the famine of the early twenties; all would have suffered its legacy. Remembering days of hunger and chaos, they preferred the peace and relatively high living standards of the post-war years to the uncertainties of today. Many see their salvation in a strong leader. Some of the survivors of Stalin's era admire him for being the only man since Peter the Great strong enough to impose order on their country.

Today the old moral certitudes have gone. A retired professor spoke for many when she said that physical hardship was nothing compared to her despair when they threatened to change the red stars on the Kremlin towers for the double-headed Tsarist eagle.

"They want to wipe out our history. Now I have to ask myself what we were trying to achieve."

Chapaevsk

"People ask me: 'What was it like?' Well I'll tell them what it was like. Where I grew up—a provincial Russian town in the middle years of this century—it made no difference which side of the barbed wire you lived on. Prisoners in camps, collective farmers, factory workers— one man's life was as bleak as another's."

C. S. WALTON: *Ivan Petrov— Russia through a Shot Glass.*

The surface conformism of Samarans masked deep political cynicism. There is no tradition of legal dissent in Russia; protest is considered futile. A group of teachers listened with incomprehension and slight shock when I spoke of strikes and demonstrations in Britain. "What do these achieve? Don't you have marches in support of your Prime Minister?" they asked, before showing me photographs of themselves on a Revolution Day parade.

"As you know, there is absolutely nowhere for us to meet socially outside our workplaces, nowhere for young people to go in the evening. Our marches gave us a day off and a chance to meet our friends. Girls brought along food, and the boys vodka. Afterwards we would drink and dance. We enjoyed those parades; the fact that we were supposed to be marching in support of the government was irrelevant."

The Gorbachev regime allowed people to organise around ecological issues. A young woman told me how she and her boyfriend had profited from this concession.

"As students we formed an ecological society called *Alternative*. It was the only cause the KGB sanctioned. I would dress in demure clothes and speak about the need to clean up the Volga. There were about 30 people in our group. On factory pay day we sent them out with collecting buckets. Misha and I pocketed every rouble. Our enterprise was good while it lasted, but it ended when the local *Komsomol* secretary began to take an interest in my book keeping.

"The activists in our group were weird. There was one old man who claimed to care passionately for wild animals and kept otters on his balcony. He would slaughter them, eat the meat, and flog the pelts. When I asked him how he could do that he replied he would go hungry if he didn't."

Eventually I met a woman who had made a serious attempt to protest against the conditions under which she was forced to live. Natasha came from Chapaevsk, a satellite town of Samara. She had brought her daughter Oksana to Samara to undergo tests at a local hospital and had dropped by to visit Boris and Lina Ivanovna.

"The town of Chapaevsk is a contaminated pit, ringed by military plants. My daughter is seriously ill. Although she is in a prestigious clinic her doctors are useless. They won't say what is wrong. They won't admit that the environment is poisoning her. It's a question of political interests. If they admitted that her illness was caused by pollution the government would have to do something about it.

"Our town would have to be placed in the high-risk category. That means we would receive some form of compensation for living there. Dimitrovgrad to the north of Samara is high-risk; they receive a better supply of scarce goods than we do, and products are cheaper. But it's easier for our local government to ignore us. We do not count. Those bureaucrats were put in their offices by Moscow and not the residents of Chapaevsk. The interests of the military are at stake.

"Goodness knows what toxins Oksana absorbed while she was a child. Many of the children in our town suffer from rashes and eczema. Chapaevsk is full of chronically sick people. Come and see for yourself."

Although only in her mid-thirties, Natasha was losing her hair. The crown of her head showed through thin strands. Later, when I met the small and frail Oksana I took her for a ten year old. She said she was 15.

I could travel to Chapaevsk without restriction providing I kept clear of its military establishments. Even local residents needed permits to approach these. On the first of May I set off with Boris as my guide. Our bus trundled out of Samara past a military airfield that was not on the map and a stadium proclaiming WORK AND SPORT ARE THE JOY OF THE PEOPLE. The Chapaevsk road led through grey concrete suburbs boasting such imaginative names as *168th Kilometre*. Then it took a straight course through bleak countryside. The oil flares of Novokuibyshevsk burned in the distant sky. Every few hundred yards the roadside was punctuated by gravestones set with red stars, marking the victims of fatal accidents.

Boris pointed to a lonely bus shelter.

"Last year a couple were attacked here by a pack of wolves. They escaped by climbing onto the roof of the shelter."

After the *Young Guard* collective farm dachaland began again. In the distance a forest of cranes ringed a monstrous building. It had the dimensions of an American shopping mall but was twice as high. "That's the new military installation that Natasha was protesting about," said Boris.

We alighted at Chapaevsk's football ground. Its wooden stands had collapsed in the middle. Crossing the Moscow-Tashkent railway track, we came upon a tiny boy crouched down, beating the rail with a stone. "There's a future gaol-bird for you. He'll grow up, get a job in a foundry, piss away his wages so his wife and children go hungry, and smash someone's face in a drunken brawl," Boris remarked in passing. Judging by what I knew of Russian family life, he may not have been overly cynical.

Five-storey *Khrushchevi* blocks stretched out into the distance on the far side of the tracks. A statue of Marx and Engels, arm-in-arm and streaked with pigeon shit, stood under the trees. Old women were rooting about in dustbins nearby.

Boris wanted to buy chocolate for Natasha's kids so we stopped off at the supermarket on the main road. It sold nothing but bread, milk and vodka. Then we investigated the farmers' market, a cluster of miserable stalls displaying only *Mars Bars*, cigarettes, and vodka. A private kiosk at the railway station offered newspapers, a book entitled *How to Catch a Husband and Keep Him*, and vodka.

Having exhausted Chapaevsk's range of commercial establishments we made our way to Natasha's flat. She lived with her husband, mother and two children in three rooms. As in most Russian homes, the living-room doubled as a bedroom. One wall was lined with books: Russian classics, Mayakovsky, and "bestsellers" translated from English. When Natasha had a spare moment she made macramé plant holders and picture frames to brighten up her rooms.

As it was a hot day and a public holiday, the family took us out for a picnic in their four-wheel-drive. An immense chemical plant lay behind their house, its chimney belching smoke into the pale sky. Beyond it a luminous green lake shimmered in the sunshine.

The car lurched across rough terrain, scattering grass snakes and gophers. A cluster of wooden shacks stood on a bluff. Windowless and half sunk into the earth, they could have been the legacy of some neglectful nineteenth century landlord, but Natasha said they were inhabited.

"A *koldoon* lives in that hut at the end. People come from far and wide for consultations. In early spring the hamlet is cut off by the flooding Volga. Every year the *koldooni* gather on the hills across the river. They claim that, outside Tibet, this is the best place for making contact with the parallel universe."

We circled back until the chimney came into view and stopped by a lake less exuberantly green than its neighbour. Natasha's 12-year-old son inflated a dinghy and paddled out to fish. With the eyes of a hunter, her husband Sasha pointed out Siberian ducks that were barely visible specks on the water.

As they brewed tea and fish soup I wandered along the lake shore. The sun blazed through the still-leafless trees. On the far bank silver birch stood black against a sky bleached white with heat. Behind them the factory chimney kept sentinel over the landscape. The grass was brown and dead underfoot. The bloated bodies of great frogs bobbed among the reeds at the water's edge. White entrails snaked from burst bellies, bringing to mind pictures of the Kurdish gas victims of Halabja.

I walked on, feeling as though I were the only living creature left on earth. Suddenly I came upon a statue of Lenin in a clearing; a colossus of greening metal that no one had bothered to take down.

As we drank tea by the lake Natasha spoke about her life in Chapaevsk.

"This town is slowly dying. There is no future for us here. They are building yet another secret weapons factory. When construction began four years ago I went to Moscow with a delegation from an ecological group. Gorbachev's aides promised to halt the building and open a sanatorium here for people suffering from respiratory diseases. Oh, they promised us medicine and all sorts of things. But it meant nothing. They continued to build.

"The new weapons plant is huge; much of it is underground. It's over there, 12 kilometres away. They are putting up workers' flats beside it. Locally, it is known as alkie city. Everyone who lives there is drunk day and night, from the soldiers who are building the plant to the officers who run it. Safety is a joke when the people in charge are off their heads.

"It's outrageous that I should need a permit to visit a friend who lives out there, when they all know my face. Yet every evening the soldiers' hostel swarms with prostitutes, and *they* don't need to show identification.

"In this town alcoholism is rampant amongst women as well as men. The military plants mainly employ women. They usually retire at 45. One place is so hazardous that workers retire after eight years. That is why they call us the city of young pensioners.

"There are several women in this town without hands. These women are former munitions assembly line workers. They put their hands through a transparent screen which protected their faces and bodies from explosions. A woman in the next block to mine lost her fingers this way.

"Over the years there have been big explosions at these factories. If you look in our town cemetery you will see the graves of the victims of those blasts. Of course the authorities tried to hush everything up.

"I shouldn't be talking to you about our military establishments; I'll tell you about the chemical plant behind our house. The factory produces household bleach and pesticides. Sasha is chief safety officer there; his job is to rescue people from gas explosions and leaks. They work with chlorine which can be dangerous.

"Work in the plant involves heavy physical labour. Much of this is performed by women. For example, they have to glue a resinous coating to the sides of metal tanks which they then fill with sulphuric acid. The factory runs 24 hours a day, on three shifts. Workers are retired at 50, 55 or 60, depending on how dangerous their particular job is.

"There is nothing good to be said of the plant. It's not a chocolate factory; there is nothing worth filching. But Sasha does get perks, such as the opportunity to buy sugar at half price.

"Almost all the workers at the plant suffer from chronic bronchitis and asthma caused by inhalation of chlorine and other chemicals. Sometimes they work in gas masks, when there is a technical fault or a leak, but this is not usual.

"Although many factories are closing we are not worried about this plant. It is true that inflation has pushed up the prices of raw materials. This means that pesticide ends up costing more than our local farms can afford. But we hear that the director of the plant has signed a contract with India and there is talk of another with America.

"During Sasha's time at the factory there has never been a serious explosion, but none of us are insured against such things. So far God has been kind to us. Pollution is the real danger. Sometimes there is a terrible smell in this town. If the wind is blowing the wrong way the local radio station broadcasts a warning. But what can we do? Sit at home with the windows shut?

"They build factories on the edge of town and we are stuck in the middle, in a contaminated pit. It feels as though they have put a ring of barbed wire around us and there is nowhere to run.

"The wildlife around here is gradually being poisoned. Sometimes Sasha catches a fish and it smells so strange we throw it away. Fish also adapt to the environment; it becomes harder and harder to find a clean one. Animals are starting to disappear from the countryside. Each year we see fewer martens and wild boar.

"For our survival we depend on the food that we grow, the fish we catch, and the animals we hunt. Everyone in Chapaevsk relies on their *dacha* for food. That's why you won't see even potatoes in the market. We Russians believe that the earth is ours; this idea predates communism. We do not buy or rent our land as you do. If we take a plot outside the town and cultivate it no one can take it away from us.

"Unfortunately over the last couple of years people have grown desperate enough to steal fruit and vegetables from each other's plots. We have put up a high fence around our *dacha*.

"In spring Sasha digs over the soil. I work all summer planting, weeding and watering. The kids help me pick cherries, apples and pears. In September Mother and I spend days salting, pickling and jam-making. Everything we have is stored in glass jars in our garage. We grow enough to see ourselves through the winter.

"The few shops in this town are virtually empty. There is a meat processing plant here and a sweet factory, but we never see their products. I don't know where they go; I expect they are sent to Moscow or even abroad.

"Nowadays our own products are being replaced by poor quality imports. In Soviet days I would buy myself a new pair of boots every three years; the following year I would buy a pair for Sasha, and then boots for the kids. These we bought several sizes too big for we knew they would last. Most families bought clothes like this, in rotation. Now we have to buy imported boots from Taiwan and Thailand, which fall apart in a season. We would rather buy Russian-made boots but we can't find them any more.

"You ask what there is to do in the evening in Chapaevsk? Nothing. We have no theatre or dance-hall, no cafés or restaurants. We used to have a cinema but that closed. Youth congregate in doorways to drink and take drugs. They are attracted to anything that is forbidden, of course. In the summer they can wander off into the woods around the city, but in winter they hang about in the stairwells of flats which are bit warmer than the street.

"I wanted to get together with some other women to start a café where we could take our children to eat ice cream. At present we have nowhere to meet except our shoe box flats. If someone comes to visit it means I have to prepare food and clean up afterwards. I wanted to go somewhere simply to sit and relax. The public bath houses used to fulfil that function, but now they build flats with bathrooms. I went to the Red Cross and to various trade unions and suggested that if families contributed a sum of money they might give us premises for a café. Not a single organisation was interested in helping."

That evening Sasha and Natasha drove us back into Samara. They exclaimed over passing Toyotas and Mercedes and slowed down to gaze at bottles of imported fruit liqueurs in kiosks. Chapaevsk made even this drab city looked like a glittering metropolis.

The next time I visited Natasha was in November. Snow lay on the ground and Sasha was preparing to go hunting. Oksana had been diagnosed as having a blood disorder and had spent the last month in hospital. I went to visit her but was not allowed into the building. Russian hospitals post dragon-ladies at the door to breathe fire on those who try to enter. They claim that germs are brought in on outdoor clothes. I had to stand on a patch of mud and shout up to Oksana's silhouetted figure at a window. Other patients had lowered buckets on string to receive food from their friends and relatives below. It seemed more like a prison than a hospital.

Back at the flat I met Natasha's mother Tamara, who came in with several loaves of bread. She had been queueing for two and a half hours in sub-zero temperatures. Everyone was stocking up as prices were due to rise the next day. They stored their loaves out on balconies, which serve as freezers in the winter.

Tamara began to talk about how good life had been in Stalin's time, when there was order in the country and food was cheap. Natasha's eyes glazed over.

In the early morning Sasha left for a day's hunting with his bloodhound. He shot duck and rabbit for food, and foxes for their fur, although he said that pelts fetched poor prices these days. Sasha found it relaxing to escape for a while into the vast whiteness. He said happiness was coming in from the cold to a glass of vodka and dinner.

But Natasha never had a day to herself.

"I am so tired. Every day I rise at six, send the kids off to school, go to work, queue for bread and milk, clean the house, and do the washing. We last had a holiday five years ago. Sasha's factory arranged a trip to Kherch on the Black Sea. The kids loved it. It was the first time any of us had seen the sea. But now life is growing harder—this drudgery never ceases.

"I work in our local children's home. With one or two exceptions, the children are not orphans. They have either been abandoned by their parents, or their mothers are in prison or deemed unfit to look after their babies. In most cases the parents are alcoholics or drug addicts who dump their children on the state. Our home is always full, but our children are the lucky ones—there are still enough places for them. Nowadays you see thousands of abandoned and runaway children living on the streets of the big cities.

"If someone is suspected of ill-treatment of their children their neighbours might denounce them to the District Committee who then send someone round to investigate. If the allegations prove to be true the children are removed and sent to us. It takes more than a few months for those parents to get their children back. If we do return them the family will continue to receive visits for several years, to make sure they are leading sober lives.

"Because of the pollution in this town the incidence of birth defects is very high. Several of our children have Down's Syndrome or are otherwise handicapped. The most seriously deformed and paralysed lie in a special hospital.

"After they leave our home at the age of three the children are sent to a boarding school. Those without developmental problems study, and then train for a profession. Once they reach eighteen they are helped to find jobs and places to live.

"It is extraordinary how many people suddenly remember their 18 year old children. Parents worry that they are growing old and decide to seek out their offspring. They go to court to obtain an order for the child to support them. Mothers say they are ill and need help. The state then pushes all obligation onto the young person's shoulders in order to relieve itself of the burden of looking after chronically ill and destitute old people.

"Imagine that, someone who never once laid eyes on their children while they were growing up suddenly starts claiming parental rights. If a woman comes to us and says she cannot afford to look after her baby she has the right to leave it with us until it is three and then reclaim it. The women who are in prison now can also reclaim their babies when they are released.

"Recently two little girls were sent to us, aged one and two. They had been left in a park with name tags on them: Lyuba and Nelly. The police found them and asked where their mother was. 'She's gone to fetch Daddy,' they replied.

"Well, they found the mother. She was only sixteen and couldn't look after her babies. I felt sorry for her, but the most important thing is to ensure the babies are cared for.

"There is a queue of people waiting to adopt our children. Last year, for example, a nice young couple came in from the country. They said they had a cow, toys, everything to offer a child. They chose a Down's Syndrome boy. Six months later they were back asking for another Down's Syndrome child. We looked at them in astonishment.

'Why don't you take a normal child?' we asked.

'We don't want the first child to feel bad when he looks at his brother and sees he is different,' they replied.

"Of course it is hard to look at these children. I feel sorry for them, poor, abandoned creatures. Still, they are better off with us than with parents who are drug addicts or alcoholics.

"The home is financed by the state. It pays for food, medicine and presents at New Year. Specialists come to us when the children are ill. They eat fruit the whole year round. The church also helps. Our old church reopened two years ago. They christen the children without charge.

"We have Russian babies, Gypsies, a little Bulgarian girl, and Kazakhs. For some reason Americans are very interested in our Kazakhs. Perhaps they mistake them for Cossacks. Not long ago a couple came to our home from America. They said they were both senators. They showed us photos of their house near Washington. They had a swimming pool, cars . . . and they wanted to adopt two Kazakh babies. I don't know why they came all the way out here to find children to adopt. They presented the home with a big bottle of aspirin and took two pretty babies away with them.

"These days it is fashionable for unmarried girls to have babies. Single mothers receive 1,000 roubles a month and move to the top of the waiting list for flats. They also have a shorter working day and better holiday arrangements. There used to be special departments in shops for them where they could buy scarce goods such as woollen underwear and tights at lower prices. There have always been a lot of single mothers around, but now girls say outright that they don't see any point in tying themselves to a husband.

"Nowadays society does not condemn them. It used to: Oh Lord, she's given birth without a husband, she's only 16, etc etc. Now it's an entirely different story. I'll give you an example: at the school where I studied there is a young teacher who wears very short skirts and high heels. She has a degree, she has an excellent qualification from the teacher training institute, and she has a child. She is unmarried. Until recently she would never have found a job as a teacher. The most important thing in those days was moral conduct, and she would have been rejected despite her qualifications. She was going to be a teacher of children, and morality is learned in school.

"I knew a couple who planned to get married. Then the girl had a son and they changed their minds. As an unmarried mother the girl was allocated a one-room flat. Of course the man has to pretend to the authorities that he does not live there. I believe a lot of young couples are doing the same thing. If I were to divorce my husband I would receive nothing for my children. The man has to pay alimony whether he likes it or not. But a single girl who gads about and gets pregnant can then go knocking at the state's door to demand her money and privileges."

Natasha took me to the children's home where she worked. It was a pleasant, sunny two-storey building ringed by a garden. About 50 babies and toddlers lived there. Five had Down's Syndrome, a few were mentally retarded and several had skin complaints, including one poor little boy with the worst case of eczema I have ever seen.

The workers in the home gathered around me to complain vehemently about their miserable wages:

"The babies here are better fed and clothed than my own. On 35,000 roubles a month I can afford nothing more than the two loaves of bread a day and two litres of milk.

"We were not well off under communism, but at least we could buy all we needed."

"We are fed up and fearful of the future. None of us bother to vote in elections. Politicians do nothing for us."

I came away from Chapaevsk stunned by its deprivation. It also left me with a lingering headache from the contaminated air.

The town exemplified the incongruity of Soviet economic development. In a sense Chapaevsk is an overgrown peasant village. Its population exist largely outside the money economy, surviving by cultivation, hunting and fishing. Yet they live in a sprawl of concrete tenements, and most adults spend their days in factories. This employment shortens their lives and causes their children to be born malformed and sick.

The residents of Chapaevsk are engaged in the production of weaponry designed to destroy people like themselves. Yet these people who operate the sophisticated technology of the armaments industry must still depend on the land for survival.

From the outside it looks as though Chapaevsk's poverty applies equally to all its citizens. Those who profit from the arms and chemical industry have not yet learned to make an ostentatious display of wealth, as they might in the West or in the larger Russian cities. The director of one of the military plants is believed to earn two million roubles a month, yet even if he has a luxury *dacha* hidden out in the country he still lives in a *Khrushchev* flat in town. Unless they travel, which they seldom do, there is nothing to which the population can compare their living standards. There are only American soaps on TV, and these come from a world so remote it might as well be another planet.

Gross incompetence is often cited as a reason for the abysmal distribution of consumer goods in provincial Russia. There are also political reasons, which become apparent in the case of categorised cities. Rather than improve industrial and environmental safety it is cheaper for the State to buy off the workforce with a few tawdry consumer items. If the population is deliberately kept at a lower-than-subsistence level they will jump at any crumbs thrown their way. Goods may be scarce but there is always vodka in the shops. Should that prove too expensive, the factories sell their employees sugar at half price which enables them to distil *samogon* in their bath tubs. Nor are those in charge much concerned if the workforce dopes itself with hashish and heroin brought in from former Central Asian republics. These anaesthetics ensure the workers' co-operation. If their heads cleared for even a few days they might question the sense of their existence. Instead they labour on for wage packets that buy more booze and narcotics.

Chapaevsk is a horrifying example of cold-blooded economic planning, where nothing was planned for the benefit of the people who had to live there. There are hundreds of Chapaevsks in Russia.

The burden of this cynical planning falls most heavily on women. Nursery schools were built so women could ruin their health in the factories. No arrangements were made to distribute fresh fruit and vegetables to the shops, so women must spend their free time tending their plots and preparing their produce for storage. There is no such thing as a launderette; women wash by hand in the bath tub. Women tend their families when they fall sick from the polluted air. There are not enough nurses in the hospitals—wages are too low—so female relatives sleep alongside their sick in the wards and corridors. This slave labour does not even merit relaxation facilities. Natasha's request that women be allowed to rent premises where they could run their own café was too unorthodox. Such initiative scared the local bureaucrats, and she was unable to raise the necessary bribes.

In Natasha's place I would have wanted to move to a more healthy environment, but mobility is discouraged. The Tsarist system of internal passports survives to this day. The first Bolshevik government abolished them as instruments of police oppression, but they were reintroduced by Stalin in 1932. These passports contain the propiski that are legally required of all

Russians. In order to obtain a *propiska* for another town a person first has to find work there.

For example, if a girl from Chapaevsk wants to move to Samara, she either takes an unpopular and low-paid job, or tries to enter one of the city's institutes. As a telephonist, tram driver or student she will gain a temporary permit. This gives her a chance to obtain permanent residency, which she usually does by marrying a Samaran.

However, in the present economic climate it will be extremely difficult for Natasha and Sasha to find work in another town. Cuts in industrial production have led to shut-downs and lay-offs all over the country. They would not leave Tamara behind. She could not support herself by nursing and has no flat of her own. They also have a well-established *dacha* which, along with Sasha's hunting and fishing forays, keep the family in food. They would face destitution if they forsook these advantages for life in a city.

Today the free market economy grants mobility to those with money. If Natasha's family had the odd 50 million roubles to spare they could buy a flat in Samara. Property prices in the cities are now almost as high as they are in Britain, but Natasha earned the equivalent of 20 pounds a month.

Most women in Chapaevsk choose to anaesthetize themselves against life. Natasha was exceptional in her conviction that things did not have to be as they were. She had tried to halt the destruction of her environment and to improve her quality of life. Tired and disillusioned, she is stuck in Chapaevsk watching her hair fall out.

The Consequences

*"The surrounding capitalist world, striving to under-
mine and disrupt the might of the USSR, worked with
redoubled energy to organize gangs of assassins, wreck-
ers and spies within the USSR . . . The Soviet Government punished these degenerates with an iron hand,
dealing ruthlessly with these enemies of the people and
traitors to the country."*

The History of the Communist Party
of the Soviet Union 1938

*"Russian servicemen and police are at the forefront of
the struggle against the most dangerous, powerful and
arrogant forces in Russian and international crime and
extremism . . . a well-spring of terrorism, ethnic tension,
drug trafficking, political extremism, a haven for criminals, a totalitarian state."*

Boris Yeltsin's Address on Chechnya,
December 1994

Russians generally see themselves as an anarchic people. On
one hand this frightens them into reverence for patriarchal
authority. Just as women believe they need the protection of a
husband, however drunken and useless, so men and women

believe their interests are best served by despotism.

On the other hand the Russian respect for political might is accompanied by a profound disregard for orders and regulations. There are Russian émigrés in London who pick up every dodge, fiddle and scam with practised ease, for they come from a culture that does not believe laws are made for the common good. The art of survival lies in learning to circumvent the rules. When every transaction is controlled by a venal bureaucracy, *blat* and bribery have more concrete meaning than illusions of democracy and civil rights.

If daily life for the majority in the post-war Soviet Union was dull and brutal, it was made bearable by a network of human support and a basic economic security. Today the former is vanishing on the heels of the latter. My neighbours in Specialist Alley think their compatriots have become cruel and greedy.

Even those who have profited from the market economy are pessimistic. Boris, Volodya and Raisa Stepanova believe their good fortune is temporary, and that the country is heading for further chaos and possible civil war.

Discontent is funnelled into the demonisation of non-Slavic "outsiders." Whenever my co-tenants thought about the causes of their immiseration they put the blame on "foreigners." Anya confessed to anti-Semitism, Boris disliked Gypsies, Tartars and Uzbeks, while a descendant of Polish settlers took me aside to whisper that "Russians are lazy, dirty, irresponsible and only understand the law of the knout."

This hatred wells up from the grinding hardship of everyday life. I came to understand this only too well for I sometimes found myself loathing the anonymous bodies that jostled me while I was out shopping. In the end, I realised the futility of raging, so I worked out a new shopping strategy. Thankfully, by the end of the day my resentment had always evaporated and my spirits been restored by the eternal kindness of my friends and neighbours.

The tragedy in Russia today is that so many people feel there is nothing they *can* do to halt their falling living standards, so they continue to seek scapegoats. By echoing the sentiments of the bread-queue and *pivnushka* nationalist demagogues reinforce this bigotry. Nationalism is spreading because it distracts attention from the cruelties imposed on the masses by those in power. As the Tsarist regime once encouraged attacks on Jews by the Black Hundreds, so today Chechen "terrorists" are made scapegoats for the plundering of Russia by the mafia and western interests.

Yet I could see that racial hatred is not the inevitable product of deprivation and insecurity. Lina Ivanovna, for example, made no distinction between nationalities; she had found kindness in a German "enemy" and cruelty in her fellow villagers. Her turbulent existence had plunged her into different ways of life, and she was intelligent enough to distinguish human qualities within these.

Unfortunately the tolerance of people like Lina Ivanovna and the *provodnitsa* Nina Mikhailovna was exceptional. Nurtured in an atmosphere of cultural and political isolation, many Samarans clung to a pathetic sense of racial superiority. Yet the apparent bigots usually had friends amongst the minorities they despised. Lina Ivanovna's son used to brag about beating up Caucasians he found hanging around the station at night. He wanted to look tough in front of the other railway police, but he spent his off-duty hours with his best friend Makar, a Georgian.

I hoped my friends and neighbours would broaden their horizons. They would not have to go far. One day I was in Lina Ivanovna's hut talking to Makar's sister Zuszanna. She laughed as she explained how her family threatened to send her back to Tblisi when she was disobedient. There she would be married off and confined to domestic work. She was enjoying herself in Samara learning German at technical school. While Zuszanna was talking Boris came in with a message. After she had gone home he said, "What a pleasant girl! I have never talked to a Georgian before. I thought they were all wild people."

But I feared it would take more than cultural mixing for my neighbours and the millions like them to shake off their nationalist sympathies. The economic crisis is too severe. In the mid-nineties the Russian government ordered foreign visitors to take AIDS tests, while they neglected domestic health education; this resurrected the old Stalinist image of a nation under threat from foreign contamination. Anti-foreigner propaganda deflects attention from the disaster inflicted on national soil by the reformers—with the help of their western advisors.

Today Russians are starting to complain that their way of life is being destroyed by western influences. Immediately after the fall of communism the country was flooded with imported western dross; nowadays they are beginning to question the extent to which *Santa Barbara* has enhanced their lives. Capitalism has proved too injurious to the mass of the population for them to be impressed by its ethos. However, in the absence of any alternative, a growing number of people are attracted by the anti-capitalist propaganda of nationalist movements.

Number Four, Specialist Alley is a microcosm of provincial Russia—a depressed and impoverished world, shot through with moments of beauty and compassion. Sadly, fear is kindling racist and authoritarian beliefs. The more scared people become the louder they clamour for strong state control. When they can no longer find refuge in the bottle or the stars, they may seek it under the centuries-old heel of despotism.

POSTSCRIPT

Despite the physical hardship of Russian life the country still attracts me more than any other and I often miss it sorely. In recent years I have visited Moscow and St. Petersburg, but have never returned to Samara. However I occasionally hear news of friends and acquaintances there. Boris married, had a child, divorced and is now back living with Nina Alexandrovna. He no longer works in the shop, but has branched out into selling tropical fish tanks to the mafia.

Lina Ivanovna has moved to a centrally-heated flat in a *micro-raion* and does not like it at all. In 1999 twenty five policemen died in a suspicious fire at the central police station. I have yet to hear if her son Alexei was among them.

In 1996 I met up with Anya while she was on holiday in London. Zoya had also been able to travel in Europe. However, the rouble crash in 1998 means it is unlikely they will be travelling anywhere in the near future.

In the late nineties the BBC showed a documentary on polluted cities in the former USSR, including Chapaevsk. It claimed 93% of the town's children were sick. I have been in touch with Sasha and Natasha. Oksana has been treated in a Moscow clinic and is doing well.

Nearly every evening there are news stories from Russia on TV. Yeltsin resigns, apartment blocks explode, war breaks out in Chechnya again, the economic situation worsens and relations with the West deteriorate. Yet through all the drama I hold a comforting picture of my former neighbours in Specialist Alley sitting drowsily around their samovars while cockroaches plod along the wainscotting and Grandad Kostya lies snoring in the corridor.

London, 2000

GLOSSARY

babushka: Grandmother, old lady.

blat: a system of power and influence.

dacha: for the majority of the population, a plot of land with a small wooden hut in one corner.

fartsovka: low-level trader, usually buying goods abroad to resell for a profit.

Khrushchev flats: public housing built during the Khrushchev years. Typically they are one, two or three-room flats in brick blocks five storeys high.

koldoon: sorceror, medicine-man.

kolkhoz: collective farm.

Komsomol: The Communist Party youth organisation.

kommunalnaya: communal flat, typically a pre-1950s apartment subdivided into one-room family flats.

kulak: wealthy peasant.

micro-raion: modern suburb of prefabricated tower blocks.

NEP (New Economic Policy): a partial market economy introduced in 1921 as a response to internal oppposition, the Tambov and Kronstadt uprisings and famine.

nomenklatura: system through which the Party controlled all access to managerial and leadership positions.

pivnushka: street kiosk selling beer.

priterpelost: the capacity to endure suffering.

propiska: registration of domicile recorded in a person's internal passport.

prostoi, prostaya: a straightforward, unpretentious man or woman.

provodnik, provodnitsa: railway carriage attendant.

samogon: home-distilled spirits.

sovkhoz: very large state farm.

spekulant: one who buys to sell for a profit.

znakharka: wise-woman, midwife and healer.

ABOUT THE AUTHOR

C.S. WALTON was born in London in 1956. She was educated at St. Paul's Girls' School and the London School of Economics. Her occupations have included pavement-painting in Berlin, house-painting in California, selling ice cream in Canada and teaching English in Brazil. She has traveled extensively in Europe, Asia and the Americas. After a visit to the USSR in 1979 she learned Russian, which helped her to establish herself in a communal flat in Samara in 1993. She was curious to find out what life had really been like behind the iron curtain.

In 1999, Garrett County Press published C.S. Walton's *Ivan Petrov: Russia through a Shot Glass*. William Brumfield, author of *Lost Russia*, said, "*Ivan Petrov* is a potent brew—part roaring, Rabelaisian tale and part social case study, with a dash of existential rebellion. This book shows, as few others have, that one of the great failings of the Soviet system was the stifling of individual initiative and the resulting sense of unbearable boredom that pervaded all social levels."

On April 19, 2000, Ms. Walton was presented with a *New London Writers Award* by the London Arts Board on the basis of *Ivan Petrov* and 10,000 words of her current work in progress on the siege of Leningrad.

She currently lives in north London.